SEASONS

LETTING GO OF THE OLD, REACHING OUT FOR THE NEW

By
Tim Gilligan

Seasons:
Letting Go of the Old, Reaching Out for the New
ISBN 0-9654627-0-6
Copyright © 2003 by Tim Gilligan
Ocala Word of Faith Church
4741 SW 20th Street
Ocala, FL 34474

Editorial Consultant: Cynthia Hansen
Text Design: Lisa Simpson

Printed in the United States of America.

DEDICATION

𝓘 dedicate this book to those "true friends" — my "big brothers and sisters" — who modeled the love and wisdom of God and were used in so many ways to help me make it into new and better "seasons of life."

To Pastor Mac and Lynne, Jane, Mike and Bonnie, Dennis and Vicki, Mylon and Christi, Keith and Phyllis, Jim and Kathleen — I am forever grateful!

Tim Gilligan

To everything there is a season,
A time for every purpose under heaven:
A time to be born, and a time to die;
A time to plant, and a time
to pluck what is planted;
A time to kill, and a time to heal;
A time to break down, and a time to build up;
A time to weep, and a time to laugh;
A time to mourn, and a time to dance;
A time to cast away stones,
and a time to gather stones;
A time to embrace,
and a time to refrain from embracing;
A time to gain, and a time to lose;
A time to keep, and a time to throw away;
A time to tear, and a time to sew;
A time to keep silence, and a time to speak;
A time to love, and a time to hate;
A time of war, and a time of peace.

— Ecclesiastes 3:1-8

TABLE OF CONTENTS

FOREWORD

*T*here are few qualities more critical to ongoing success than proper perspective. Whether that perspective involves our past or our present, our ability to view the circumstances and situations of life through the right "lens" is at the heart of godly wisdom. Having a proper perspective helps us not only know *what* to do, but even more importantly, it helps us know *when* to do it.

My good friend and fellow pastor, Tim Gilligan, has demonstrated this quality of maintaining the proper perspective in both his life and ministry. Now in this insightful and revealing book, he provides all of us with a framework for doing the same in our lives.

Launching from the simple but timeless truth, "to everything there is a season" (Eccl. 3:1), Tim reveals how viewing life through the "seasons lens" releases us to discover and fulfill our divine destiny. I thank him for providing a practical yet powerful structure to help us get unstuck from our past, learn the lessons of the present, and capture the potential of our future in God.

I encourage you to open your heart and mind to this new "lens" for viewing your life. It will supply you with the proper perspective, which will in turn open to you a world of new opportunities and enable you to become a successful navigator of the diverse challenges and seasons of life.

Mac Hammond, Pastor
Living Word Christian Center
Minneapolis, Minnesota

INTRODUCTION

A few years ago, my wife Alicia's grandfather came to visit us from his German village of Hohenpeissenberg, located way up in the Austrian Alps. One thing is for sure — there are no Wal-Marts in Hohenpeissenberg! So it was quite an experience for the elderly gentleman when his granddaughter took him to a grocery store for the first time.

His first surprise came when he walked up to the store and the doors opened by themselves. But he was absolutely overwhelmed when he walked in and saw the rows and rows of food items that filled the store — not to mention the housewares, automotive supplies, paper products, and a whole host of other things! The elderly man just wandered up and down the aisles, gazing in wonder at the sheer variety and abundance of available goods, never once thinking to touch anything or choose an item to put in the shopping basket.

Many people wander through life like Alicia's grandfather wandered through that store. They never decide what they want or what they *don't* want to keep as a part of their lives. Instead, they just accept whatever comes their way as "the way things are," wondering all the while why the bad always seems to outweigh the good.

That *isn't* the way God intends for us to live. He wants to take us from glory to glory! In His plan, our path is to shine ever brighter until that perfect day (Prov. 4:18). But all too often we put ourselves on "auto-pilot" and allow ourselves to just cruise through life without considering where we're going or what we're missing because of our own complacency.

It is time for us to wake up and pay attention to what is happening in our lives. We need to start deliberately choosing what we want to keep and what we want to get rid of instead of wandering through life with a dazed look on our faces!

This is exactly what God's message is to us in His Word:

> **And do this, knowing the time, that now it is high time to awake out of sleep; for now our salvation is nearer than when we first believed.**
> **The night is far spent, the day is at hand....**
>
> **Romans 13:11,12**

> **Live life, then, with a due sense of responsibility, not as men who do not know the meaning and purpose of life but as those who do. Make the best use of your time, despite all the difficulties of these days.**
>
> **Ephesians 5:15,16[1]**

---

[1] J. B. Phillips, *The New Testament in Modern English* (New York: MacMillan Co., 1966), p. 429.

We would do well to heed these divine warnings. However, we can't leave behind the defeats of the past and choose a better future for ourselves until we understand an all-important concept: *Life on this earth is made up of seasons.*

Why is this understanding so important? Because without it, we lock ourselves into our past and present circumstances. We say things like, "I can't hold down a job"; "Things never work out for me"; or "I just don't think I can do this. Every time I've ever tried in the past, I've failed."

But it doesn't matter *what* bad things have happened in our past. It doesn't matter if we just received a bad report from our doctor, our banker, a friend or family member, our employer, or our stockbroker. Whatever comes our way, we can rest in the knowledge that no past defeat or bad report has to define our entire lives. *It is just a season!*

So how do we escape the undesirable seasons we've been trapped in for so long? We'll find the answer to that question in the Word of God. The Scriptures tell us how to get out of a season, how to extend a season, how to preserve good things from one season to the next, and how to be delivered from bad things that should be left behind. This is the information we *must* have if we're ever going to learn how to navigate successfully through each season of our lives.

That's what we're going to talk about in this book. We'll discuss how we can perpetuate and increase the blessings God desires for us to carry from season to season. However, our first order of business will be to get rid of the hindrances that have kept us stuck for too long in an old season. Only then will we be able to move on into the good future God has planned for us.

I'm excited about this message on the seasons of life, because I didn't pull it together from a collection of abstract, theoretical truths I found in the Bible. These are life-changing principles that the Lord has personally ministered to me in the car, in the shower, and in all kinds of places as I've gone about my daily business.

I feel a great responsibility to make sure I'm a faithful steward of this message. Therefore, whenever the Lord put something on my heart regarding the subject of seasons, I tracked it down in the Scriptures and verified that the Word bears witness to its truth. Now it's my prayer that God would minister these powerful truths to your heart as He has so faithfully done for me.

So get ready to embrace a new season, friend. There has never been a better time than now to step out of that old season once and for all and enter into a better future that shines ever brighter unto the perfect day!

Tim Gilligan

GOD'S PLAN FOR YOU: A FUTURE AND A HOPE

1

S olomon was about to assume the throne of his father David, and he knew he needed help. So when the Lord appeared to Solomon one night and asked him what he desired most, the young man asked for only one thing: divine wisdom to help him lead the nation of Israel. Pleased with Solomon's answer, God granted his request. In fact, Solomon went on to become the wisest man who ever lived!

It's important to understand this about Solomon, because he discovered a crucial key to understanding the ways of God during his unparalleled pursuit of wisdom. We're going to focus on that key as we talk about what we can do to walk in the fullness of God's good plan for our lives. It is found in Ecclesiastes 3:1:

> **To everything there is a season, a time for every purpose under heaven.**

The principle is simple but profound: *As we pass through life on this earth, we're going to pass through seasons.*

13

Solomon went on to list some of the seasons we all go through in different ways and for different reasons:

- A time to be born, and a time to die.
- A time to plant, and a time to pluck what is planted.
- A time to break down, and a time to build up.
- A time to weep, and a time to laugh.
- A time to mourn, and a time to dance.
- A time to cast away stones, and a time to gather stones.
- A time to embrace, and a time to refrain from embracing.
- A time to gain, and a time to lose.
- A time to keep, and a time to throw away.
- A time to tear, and a time to sew.
- A time to keep silence, and a time to speak.
- A time to love, and a time to hate.
- A time of war, and a time of peace.

Solomon's list of seasons is obviously a partial one; however, we can see that he included a number of negative things. There is good reason for that. As long as we live in this natural realm, we will all have to deal with circumstances that we're not real thrilled about. But whenever bad things happen to us, Solomon gives us the key for dealing with their negative effects — *we must seek to understand the times and seasons of our lives.*

GOD'S PLAN OF PEACE FOR YOU

How do you begin the process that leads to this understanding? First, you have to know beyond a shadow of a doubt that God is a *good* God and that He is thinking only good thoughts toward you. Jeremiah 29:11 confirms this:

For I know the thoughts that I think toward you, says the Lord, thoughts of peace and not of evil, to give you a future and a hope.

Get hold of this scripture, for it's the Lord who is speaking here. He is saying what He intends for you and what He is thinking about you. And the bottom line is this: God has only *good* things planned for you. His thoughts, intentions, and plans are only of peace, not of evil. You have to plant that thought deep in your heart if you ever want to enter into the future and the hope that God has laid out before you.

The Hebrew word *shalom* is translated "peace" in this verse, and it means *safe, well, happy, friendly, welfare, health, peace,* and *prosperity.*[2] It also carries the idea of *nothing missing* or *nothing broken.* This is the peace that surpasses all natural understanding, the peace that guards your heart and mind in Christ (Phil. 4:7). You have to grasp the fact that this is what God intends for you, even if the definition for *shalom* doesn't yet exclusively describe your life.

God is not the author of your trouble. Right now He is thinking thoughts of peace and not evil about you. By definition, that word "evil" means *bad, adversity, affliction, calamity, distress, misery, sorrow, grief, trouble, undoing,* and *misfortune.*[3] This is definitely *not* a description of what God has planned for your life!

---

[2] James Strong, "Hebrew Dictionary of the Old Testament," *The Exhaustive Concordance of the Bible* (Iowa Falls, Iowa: Riverside Book and Bible House), #7965.

[3] Ibid., #7451.

You probably have some circumstances in your life right now that would fit the definition of "evil." And if you don't have any right now, trust me — you'll have some later on down the road. All of us face adverse circumstances to some extent at one time or another.

But if you *are* experiencing anything that can be categorized as evil, don't just accept it as something you have to live with the rest of your life — because you *don't*! Refuse to drag it along with you from this season to the next. Instead of saying, "This is my life," begin to declare, "This is just a season!"

You have to keep on moving forward, leaving behind the seasons God never intended for you to go through in the first place. Where are you going? To the better future God says He has already planned for you. Your part is to hold fast to your hope about the future that God is waiting to unfold before your eyes.

The word "hope" has to do with *confident expectation*. That's a quality many people no longer possess. Somewhere along the way, they lost their expectation for a better future. As a result, they also lose out on the future God ordained for them to walk in before they were ever born.

Don't let that happen to you. You do have a future. You do have a hope. You are not hemmed in or locked in to where you are right now. It isn't a matter of "this far and no further." God wants to keep you moving toward your future and your hope. There is a divine purpose filled with peace and wholeness and prosperity that you have yet to fulfill!

> You are not hemmed in or locked in to where you are right now.

'IN THE WORLD
YOU HAVE TRIBULATION'

Of course, that doesn't mean you will never experience any problems. That won't happen until you get to Heaven! Don't let anyone tell you that Christians aren't supposed to have any problems. The truth is, when you become a Christian, you face a whole new set of problems that you never dealt with before you got saved!

We may as well face it — while we're on the earth, we *will* have challenges. Jesus confirmed this in John 16:33 (*AMP*) when He said, "*...In the world you have tribulation and trials and distress and frustration....*"

I once listened to a Christian song that talked about the devil not bothering us anymore. I had to listen carefully to make sure it wasn't talking about dying and going home to be with the Lord, because that's the only way the devil won't bother us any longer! As long as we are on this earth, we will have tribulations, trials, frustrations, and distress. But Jesus also gave us a magnificent promise in that same verse:

> **...But be of good cheer [take courage; be confident, certain, undaunted]! For I have overcome the world. [I have deprived it of power to harm you and have conquered it for you.]**

Jesus has deprived the world of its power to harm us! I'm very thankful for that divine promise. Thank God, His desire is to deliver us out of undesirable seasons into new seasons of blessing and increase! Therefore, I plan on enjoying my life, and I look forward to my future — and you need to do the same!

We can only begin to look forward to our future when we understand that some things we experience are *not* what God has planned for us. We need to separate God's good plans from the bad things that come into our lives through a variety of openings.

The main reason we experience heartache in our lives is that we have an enemy who absolutely hates our guts. You see, we remind the devil of God. We were created in God's image. God has "wired" us with gifts, callings, and anointings that reside within us, whether or not we are actually using them. The enemy sees the God-potential in us, and he hates it with a passion. Therefore, he is always looking for ways to steal, kill, and destroy everything good in our lives.

One of the enemy's favorite tricks is to convince you to assign your problems to *your life* instead of to *the current season*. Maybe you messed up or lost out on a blessing during a particular season. Perhaps you got sick, some things didn't go well for you, or you failed in some way. Whatever problem you struggled with, the devil wants you to assign it to your whole life, not just to that season. He wants you to see yourself as a loser or a "wanna-be." He wants the problem that is hindering you in the present season to continue limiting you for the rest of your life.

However, we can't blame the devil for everything. The truth is, we run into some negative circumstances just because we live on planet earth. Other times we experience problems because none of us have a perfect walk with God, and we forget that we don't get sand spurs when we stay on the sidewalk. In other words, we take a wrong turn that creates a mess!

What do I mean by a wrong turn? Sometimes we lack wisdom. Sometimes we're careless. Sometimes we're rebellious. Sometimes we don't follow all the way through on our responsibilities. Sometimes a situation isn't clear to us, and we make a wrong decision that gets us moving in an entirely different direction.

Most of us know what it's like to miss an exit while driving down the highway. We think, *Wow! I just missed my turn, and the next exit is a hundred miles down the road!* Then we start studying the median, trying to figure out a way to cut across without getting stuck or arrested!

Well, we "miss exits" in life as well, and it's important to identify the times we've made that mistake. Once we do that, we can begin looking for a way to turn around and backtrack so we can get on the right road according to *God's* direction for our lives.

Finally, there are times that bad things happen because some of the people who surround us in life choose to be careless, selfish, insensitive, or disobedient. Their lives bump into ours, and the consequences for their wrong choices spill over and affect us adversely.

Whatever the source of our problems, it is so important that we grasp the principle that Solomon discovered: *Our lives are lived in seasons.* And it is God's plan and design that we leave behind in a past season the negative things that are not of Him.

We see this principle consistently presented in the Scriptures. Over and over again, God tells us that He wants to deliver us from any bad place we find ourselves in — even if that bad place was the result of our own making — so He can bring us to a place of abundance and blessing.

God is a delivering God, and He delivers you out of the pit, even if you dug the pit! His desire and intention for you is to give you a future and a hope. He is thinking thoughts toward you of peace and not of evil. He loves you. He has planned wonderful things for you on the road ahead.

Yes, you have an enemy; you may be rebellious or foolish at times; and you may have made mistakes and wrong choices in the past. And as a result of all these things, you may sometimes deal with undesirable consequences in your life. In fact, you may be experiencing a season of loss, failure, or rebellion right now. But that doesn't have to label you for life. You can leave those negative things behind in the old season where they originated.

> God is a delivering God, and He delivers you out of the pit, even if you dug the pit!

Unfortunately, people often don't resolve negative things that arise within a season, and as a result, they allow those things to affect their entire lives. *I was a loser in this situation,* they think, *and I'll probably be a loser for the rest of my life.*

But that is never God's plan for us. We were all stinky old sinners at some point, but through the blood of Jesus, we're free from all that! Now God wants to take us from glory to glory. He wants to move us into the next season of our lives!

LIVING IN THE REALM OF TIME

So just what do we mean when we talk about seasons? The word "seasons" refers to a period of time, and *time* refers to the space between two eternities of timelessness.

You see, eternity never had a beginning. It has always been, and it will continue on without end. The same is true of God. He is the Alpha and the Omega, the Almighty One who has no beginning and no end.

The Bible says that God has also set eternity in the hearts of men (Eccl. 3:11). In other words, we don't just vanish when our lives on this earth are over; we enter into eternity. That means we are in training right now, and eternity is the "north" on our spiritual compass. As we respond correctly to the life-giving Word of God by becoming children of God, our hearts are directed into the right eternity, where we will rule and reign with Him forever.

Meanwhile, however, we are finite beings who live within a sliver called *time*, wedged between two eternities. That makes it difficult for us to understand an eternal God who never began to exist. After all, time was a factor for us from the moment of our birth, when the nurse wrote down the time we popped out! And time will continue to be a factor throughout our stay on this earth — right up to the moment when someone writes down the hour and the minute we check out of this life.

It is our lot to wear the shackle of time in this life. Consider the Sunday morning church service as an example. There is a certain time that the service starts. After a while, the pastor runs out of time and sends the people home, many of whom are also watching their watches because they need to take the roast out of the oven, watch their favorite football team on television, etc. The truth is, we may try to decorate time and make it look pretty, but it nevertheless remains a shackle that ties us to this natural realm.

As long as we live on this earth, we have to work within a framework of time that is divided into years, seasons, months, weeks, days, hours, and minutes. God spoke forth these divisions of time when He first created the heavens and the earth:

> **Then God said, "Let there be lights in the firmament of the heavens to divide the day from the night; and let them be for signs and seasons, and for days and years."**
>
> **Genesis 1:14**

For our purposes, we are going to divide time only into seasons. I'm not referring to the literal seasons of winter, spring, summer, and fall, but rather to the seasons that mark certain periods of time in our lives. We want to make sure we understand the times and the seasons of our lives the best we can; otherwise, we stand in danger of missing out on the purpose God has called us to fulfill on this earth.

From our human perspective, time is a very relative concept. For instance, two weeks of vacation is a whole lot different than two weeks on a diet! And when people come to visit us, some can stay longer in one hour than others can stay in a week!

When we enjoy what we're doing, time flies. When we are not enjoying ourselves, time slows to a maddening crawl. We certainly know that's true when we tell our children to do their homework!

The child protests, "But I have a lot of homework! I don't want to do it all now!"

The parent says, "Well, go work on some of it right now."

"For how long?"

"Work on your homework for at least twenty minutes."

So the child goes to his room to work on homework. Two minutes later, he's back, asking, "Has it been twenty minutes yet?"

"No, it's only been *two* minutes," the parent replies, "and you spent half of that time walking to your room!"

But it's an entirely different matter when we cut our children loose to go play. They can just go on and on forever when they're doing what they want to do!

USING YOUR 'CURRENCY' WISELY

Time is the currency of this dimension. That makes it extremely valuable — so valuable, in fact, that everyone is trying to get some of yours!

Most of us are actually better stewards of our money than of our time. If someone comes up to us and asks, "Do you have a minute?" we don't think much of it. But if someone asks us if we have ten dollars he can borrow, we take that seriously!

However, we have it backwards. Our time is much more valuable to us than our money, and we need to guard it zealously. According to Psalm 90:12, we have to learn how to weigh out our time and use it in the proper way:

So teach us to number our days, that we may gain a heart of wisdom.

"To number" means *to weigh out* or *to measure*.[4] It can also carry the meaning of *to make good use of*. As you begin to number your days and make good use of your time, you begin to gain wisdom — and that is the greatest thing you could ever gain. As Proverbs 4:7 says, *"Wisdom is the principal thing...."*

"I just need more money." No, you just need more wisdom. "I need friends. I need a break. I need more time." No, in actuality, what you need is wisdom.

You need to continually remind yourself that God's wisdom is the primary thing you need in this life. You can come out of any bad season if you will choose to number your days and use your time wisely so your life can bring benefit and blessing to the Kingdom of God.

I endeavor to use my time wisely even with my ministry staff members. Sometimes they'll come to me and ask, "Do you have a minute?"

I'll respond, "I have half a minute."

What do I mean when I say that? I'm on track. I'm trying to use my time wisely because it's valuable to me, and I want others to value it as well. That message causes my staff members to be precise rather than to take four hours and twenty-eight minutes in a meeting to discuss something we could zero in on in a fraction of the time.

---

[4] Ibid., # 4487.

We should be glad to give our time to others, but we still have to be very cautious about how we use our time. We must also be considerate of how we use other people's time. For instance, if we call people on the telephone, we need to realize that they probably weren't sitting around waiting for our phone call! Instead of just plowing right in and starting a conversation with them before they have a chance to say anything, we should be considerate enough to ask, "Is this a good time?"

Since time is the currency of this dimension, it has to be spent. There are all sorts of books, tapes, and self-help resources available on the market to tell you how to save time. But the truth is, you *can't* save time; you can only become more efficient with it. I mean, you can't store extra minutes in a storage box so that when it's time to go on vacation, you have seventeen extra hours saved for a special occasion!

Some people have no purpose and no focus, and time just passes them by, day after day. They never use their time to any benefit; they never realize that they are wasting the true currency of this dimension. Time is their most valuable possession, but they'll never get back what they have already squandered as days turn into months and months turn into years.

Proverbs 12:11 (*TLB*) says, *"Hard work means prosperity; only a fool idles away his time."* What do fools do? They idle away time. How do they become wise? They begin to number and measure their days, and they gain a heart of wisdom.

Ephesians 5:15,16 says, *"See then that you walk circum-spectly, not as fools but as wise, REDEEMING THE TIME, because the days are evil."* That word "circumspectly" carries the meaning of *circular, all around,* or *on all sides.* In other words, we are to walk through life seeing all sides and acutely aware of what is around us.

That's a good description of the way you have to drive a vehicle in order to be safe. You need to stay aware of what is around you, so it's important that you keep your windshield clear and use your rearview and side view mirrors. You certainly *don't* rip your rearview or your side view mirrors off your car or let your windshield get so dirty that you can't even see out of it!

You have to be able to see where you are going and what's going on around you. That isn't being paranoid; it's just being wise about how you drive a car.

Look at what verse 16 says again: *"...redeeming the time, because the days are evil."* The implication here is that if we don't redeem the time — if we don't make the best of the opportunities and events that come our way — our days will become evil or hurtful.

This especially applies to our spiritual walk. For instance, we should make the best use of our time whenever we go to church. We have already set apart that time to worship with other believers, so it only makes sense that we would make that time count. If we just sit in the pew and study the hairdo in front of us instead of getting hold of what God has for us, we might miss out on a revelation that is exactly what we need to prepare for the next season in our lives.

A FRESH START
EVERY MORNING

But here's the great thing about time: Every one of us is given a fresh stack of twenty-four hours every day because of God's infinite mercy!

Lamentations 3:22,23 tells us that His mercies are new every morning. So we all get a fresh start, a brand-new chance. Even if we wasted time yesterday, even if we wasted *all* of yesterday, even if we are chronic time-wasters — God still gives us twenty-four more hours to use wisely and profitably.

So with every new dawn, God slides twenty-four more hours across the table as if it were currency and makes you the steward of that time. Your job is to use it very wisely and to manage those twenty-four hours for the purpose of increase. You are *not* to just carelessly let those hours come and go without any thought or effort on your part. You are to take the time given to you and work hard with it.

Some people are locked into the mindset that they cannot get a grip on time. But in reality, they have the same fresh start every day that everyone else does.

I really like that concept of a fresh start. When I was in elementary school, my behavior in class resulted in the teacher writing my name on the chalkboard pretty regularly. So it made me feel good when I'd come into class the next morning and see that someone had washed the chalkboard clean. My name, along with the five or six check marks after it, would be gone, and I'd have a fresh start!

That was definitely a good feeling. But it's much more wonderful to realize that God's mercies are new every morning as I seek to follow His plan for my life!

SPENDING TIME
WITH THE TIMELESS ONE

Time is life, and how we spend our time is how we spend our life. Therefore, the wisest thing we can do is spend time with the Timeless One. That *doesn't* mean we should try to find some leftover time to give God out of our busy days.

Typically we all run out of time each day. What do we say about those unfinished projects around the home? "I just don't have the time." Or when our kids want to go somewhere, we often respond, "I wish we could, but we don't have the time."

> ...The wisest thing we can do is spend time with the Timeless One.

But we can't live our relationship with God in a perpetual deficit status. If we do, our relationship with Him will eventually become bankrupt. We have to *make* time to spend with the Timeless One.

If you want to walk in wholeness and blessing and victory, the wisdom of this world won't do you any good. You have to gain true wisdom, and that only comes from above. It literally comes out of eternity, and there is only one way to obtain it — by spending time with God.

You can spend that time in prayer, in the Word, or in worshiping the Lord. There are also times when you just have to be still before Him and know that He is God. But no matter how you spend your time with Him, don't do it with your leftovers. Give the Lord the firstfruits of your time.

As you do, a divine transaction will take place. You will give God the currency of this dimension — your time — and in return you will receive out of eternity the wisdom, revelation, and strength you need. And when the transaction is complete, you will come out of that place of intimate fellowship both refreshed and transformed.

Recently I realized that it was time for me to set aside some quality time to spend with the Lord. Some precious church members allowed me to use their vacation condominium, located right next to the ocean on a beautiful, relaxing Florida beach.

Every morning and afternoon, I'd walk for an hour on the beach, pondering the vastness of the ocean and how small I am in comparison. At night I would open the sliding doors of my fourth-floor condo and let the sound of the waves and the ocean breeze roll in.

My stay at that beach was wonderful. I'm spoiled now. I think I'll have to buy a "sounds of the ocean" CD; then I'll turn on the fan while my wife sprays water on me!

Several times I walked barefoot to the dock and leaned against a pole at the water's edge as the tide was coming in, enjoying the cool feeling of the water splashing in and the sand slipping out from underneath my feet. I'd just stand there and not even think. It was as if someone took the top off my head and let it air out for a while. (We all need quiet experiences like that every once in a while. Otherwise, our minds get a little moldy and don't work as quickly.)

One time I was leaning against this pole, feeling the waves coming in and the sand going out from under my feet, watching the birds flying overhead and feeling the breeze blowing on my face. I had been there awhile, just being still, when all of a sudden I became acutely aware of God's presence. I felt so close to Him both at that moment and throughout my stay at the beach, which was the very reason I set aside that time in the first place.

Of course, you can't live your entire life like that, away from the normal responsibilities of life. But you *can* make spending time alone with God a part of your life. Set aside quality time to fellowship with the Lord each day in the Word and in prayer. Take the time to get still before Him so that you can come to know that He is God in *your* life.

SIX POINTS TO REMEMBER ABOUT SEASONS

How we relate to and deal with the seasons of our lives will determine the quality of our lives. Therefore, the following six principles about seasons are important ones to grasp:

1. *We don't want to get stuck in a season.*

I've seen people in their fifties who still think of themselves as the ninth-grade track star or the high school prom queen. They are stuck in a season that they should have left long ago.

In the natural realm, we sometimes get stuck in certain seasons of styles and fashions. For instance, young people today are wearing clothes that their parents threw away or buried in bunkers!

My mom didn't let me buy platform shoes until that style of shoes was on its way out. Finally she relented; *finally* I could be cool. But when I showed up in my platform shoes, I found out quickly that they weren't cool anymore. Suddenly I was trying hard to hide the fact that I was an extra six inches tall!

Today many of the fashions of the '70s are back. As for those platform shoes, some entrepreneur must have held on to a bunch of them, because they're back out on the shelves again and young people are buying them!

This is a frivolous illustration, but the principle is anything *but* frivolous. You have to make sure that you don't get stuck in a season. If you have been going through a season of grief, failure, or loss, don't stay there. You can come out of it!

Whatever has happened to you in the past, no matter how unfortunate it was, you need to leave it in that season. If you drag it with you through life, it will create all kinds of problems for you. For one thing, you could easily become codependent and dysfunctional in your relationships with others.

But God has called you to be free! You are called to be blessed and to be a blessing — to *enjoy* this life, not just to "grin and bear it." And to make sure you *don't* get stuck in a season and lose out on His good plan for your life, God even gives you "daily supplements" from Heaven in the form of peace, joy, and help from above. All these blessings are yours to claim as a child of God.

So if a tree falls on you in a certain season, don't just lie there. Kick that tree off of you! If it's too big to kick off, chew on it till it's smaller. Light it on fire. Do *something* to get rid of whatever is holding you down so you can get out of that season and move on!

2. *We don't want to miss a season.*

Another definition for the Hebrew word *moed*, which is translated "season" in Genesis 1:14, is *an appointment* or *a fixed time.*[5] The concept of time carries the meaning of a period of duration with boundaries. It has limits, but it continues to pass and to advance.

As I was pondering this definition of "season," the Lord ministered this principle strongly to my heart: *Since a season is an appointment, you have to be cautious regarding "disappointments."*

If you experience a disappointment and you don't handle it right, a disappointment can cause you to miss your divine appointment. If that happens, you have to make sure you get "reappointed" to the season you missed and the divine assignment you were to fulfill.

Be very careful how you handle any disappointments that come your way. Don't ever let yourself say again, "My life is just full of disappointments" or "I'm just one great big disappointment." When you develop that kind of mindset, your disappointments will cause you to miss the next appointment or season God has for you.

I've seen that happen many times. People take a wrong turn. Maybe they make a wrong decision, fail in some way,

---

[5] Ibid., #4150.

or are unwilling to do something God has instructed them to do. Perhaps an undesirable circumstance arises in their lives that they weren't planning on, or an endeavor that is important to them doesn't work out.

Whatever the cause for the wrong turn, these people get so laden down with the disappointment that they can't move forward any longer and, as a result, they miss their next season or appointment. They end up living the rest of their lives in the gray zone of disappointment, never realizing their potential in God.

God doesn't want that to happen to us. He designed life on this earth not to be merely endured, but to be *enjoyed*. Remember, Jesus told us in John 10:10 (*AMP*) the reason He came to redeem us — so we could *"...have and enjoy life, and have it in abundance (to the full, till it overflows)"*!

3. *We should never fail to reap a harvest from every season.*

We see this principle demonstrated in the book of Exodus. The children of Israel had been held as slaves in captivity for 430 years under Egyptian rule. But one day the Lord spoke to them through Moses that He was preparing to deliver them, giving them this promise to hold on to: *"And I will give this people favor in the sight of the Egyptians; and it shall be, when you go, that you shall not go empty-handed"* (Exod. 3:21).

For 430 years, the Israelites had been treated like dirt — pushed down, held back, and abused in every possible way. But the Lord declared that they wouldn't leave empty-handed from the nation that had oppressed them so grievously. He gave them so much favor that they actually plundered the Egyptians without a fight!

"Can I have all your silver and gold? Can I have all your nice stuff? Can I have your SUV and your trailer too?" And the Egyptians said, "Sure, take whatever you want. Just *go!*"

It had been a long, dark season of captivity and hardship for the Israelites; nevertheless, they did not leave Egypt empty-handed. Instead, they left *the Egyptians* empty-handed as they went forth to a new season of freedom on their way to the Promised Land!

You should always gain something of benefit from *anything* you go through. Even if the season you are just coming out of is a coma, you should at least come out rested! There is always something you can gain, no matter how unpleasant a season has been. You should come out with a greater revelation of God's Word. You should come out with a lesson learned. You should come out with a greater appreciation of God's faithfulness.

> You should always gain something of benefit from *anything* you go through.

Even if you're going through a season that you wish would get done in a hurry, you can still come out of that season with a greater trust in God because He has just delivered you out of a pit. It may have been bad, but think how much worse it would have been without God on your side!

It is this principle that enables you to tap into God's promise in Proverbs 4:18: *"But the path of the just is like the shining sun, that shines ever brighter unto the perfect day."* Not only should your path shine ever brighter, but *you* should be brighter than you used to be. You should come out of every season a little wiser than before. As one minister put it, even an old, blind pig will find an acorn now and then if he works at it!

You need to come out of every situation with greater faith, greater trust, and a greater heart of gratitude. You need to come out with lessons learned and an added measure of wisdom gained from experience. When you go through a season God's way, you will always come out a little more seasoned than you were before. And what you gain and bring out of that season will help you in your next season.

But make sure you don't come out of a season with just any kind of harvest; it has to be the *right* harvest. Don't bring out a bad attitude or a root of bitterness. Don't bring out an attitude of "Woe is me! How pitiful I am!" You're not pitiful; you're coming *out* — and you're not coming out empty-handed!

Some people keep repeating the same foolish mistakes, going around the same mountain again and again but never reaching their destination. You don't ever have to fit in that category. As you determine to gain something good from each season of your life, you will go from faith to faith, as the apostle Paul talks about in Romans 1:17. You will grow ever stronger in faith. Your testimony won't sound like the testimony of many Christians who say, "Well, three years ago I was strong in God, but I'm not now" or "I used to be really close to God. I used to serve Him and love Him with all my heart."

Do you know why so many Christians say things like that? Because they let a season get the best of them rather than making sure *they* got the best out of *the season*!

Don't ever let that be a description of you. Determine to grow ever brighter and stronger in faith as you pass through the seasons of life!

4. *We should enjoy what we can in every season.*

Some seasons are much easier to enjoy than others, but you should always look for ways to enjoy every season of life that you go through. Of course, you will experience some seasons that seem like spring and fall. When you go through that kind of season, you sense that change is in the air. The weather is different. Everything feels fresh and alive; the view seems more colorful and beautiful. Circumstances in your life are wonderful, and everything seems to be going your way.

But you will also experience seasons that feel much more like winter. These are the times you have to deliberately look for ways to enjoy life in the midst of circumstances that seem barren and cold.

When some people are going through a season that is bitterly cold, they choose to become cold and bitter themselves. These people always want to shiver and complain about how cold it is.

But I'll tell you what you should do. First, accept the fact that you're going through a cold season. Second, go outside and chop some wood. Keep on working even if your fingers and nose get numb. Then take that wood inside, build a cozy fire, pull up an easy chair, and thaw out with a hot cup of cocoa!

You might also go through a season where circumstances seem so hot that you can hardly find any relief from the heat. After standing around for just a few minutes, even your socks are wet with sweat!

Well, there are some things you can do to enjoy that season as well. Drink some icy lemonade. Then peel off those sweaty socks and dive into a cool lake! I'm telling you, friend, there is something to enjoy in *every* season, no matter how unpleasant it seems to be!

5. *We don't want to grow weary of doing good in the midst of a season.*

There will also be some seasons in your life when you feel like you're peddling your bike all the way up a very steep hill.

Where I come from, if you walk your bike up the hill, you are a sissy. So you figure out a way to ride your bike all the way up that hill, even if you have to come back down a second time and get a running start so the momentum can help push you all the way to the top. Only when you've made it to the top can you afford to relax and coast for a while.

A lot of people want to peddle just a little bit in these "uphill" seasons. Then when it starts getting a little more difficult, they just want to stop peddling altogether and let their bike slow to a stop.

But you can't go through those seasons sitting on the bike seat; you have to stand up and peddle *hard* in order to keep moving forward. In other words, you have to not only keep on doing the right things, but you have to do them with *energy*. That's how you fulfill God's command in Galatians 6:9:

> **And let us not grow weary while doing good, for in due season we shall reap if we do not lose heart.**

If you don't lose heart, if you don't cave in, if you don't give up and quit — *then* you will reap a harvest of blessing from the season you're going through, no matter how difficult that season is. But you have to continue to do the right thing, and you can't grow weary in doing it. Weariness gives you the temptation to quit at a time when pressing on toward the next season matters the most.

This is a big problem in the Body of Christ at large today. So many Christians are doing the right thing, but they are *not* doing the right thing with energy.

You cannot grow weary in doing good if you want to get out of an undesirable season. You have to apply some energy to moving those obstacles that stand in your way, and you have to release your faith by speaking and acting on what you believe. God promises that you will reap a good harvest in due season if you don't quit, faint, or become paralyzed with disappointment.

6. *We should monitor our seasons.*

In reality, we go through a mix of seasons simultaneously in life. We are never in just one season.

You have several different seasons going on in your life right now. If you have children, your relationship with them is in a certain season. At the same time, you may be going through an entirely different season in your finances, in your health, or in a host of other areas of your life.

There are some things that overlap and are carried over from season to season. Other things remain constant through all the seasons of your life. It is your responsibility to monitor your seasons and make sure anything that is carried over to the next season is positive. Don't let yourself carry past garbage — bad attitudes, hurts, offenses, sinful habits, and so forth — into the next season of your life.

That's why you can never stop paying attention or monitoring the seasons in your life. You have to stay alert and spiritually awake at all times, working hard while trusting God to order your steps. Don't just walk through life without making any effort to understand the times and seasons of your life. You need to be very purposeful in how you live.

Ask yourself, *Where am I right now? What is in my life that is not part of God's plan for me?* If you identify things in your life that shouldn't be there, don't let those negative things define your life — *assign them to a season.* Then refuse to let that season go on forever. Start looking for the exit door, and get out of there in a hustle!

> If you identify things in your life that shouldn't be there, don't let those negative things define your life — *assign them to a season.*

'THIS IS JUST A SEASON!'

It's our choice to make. Society has sold us a bunch of lies that can easily keep us trapped in old seasons if we accept those lies as truth. We can hold on to the mindset that says, "We're poor, and we've always been poor. We're ignorant, and we've always been ignorant." But the truth is, we don't have to stay trapped in those seasons that society has imposed on us. We don't have to buy those lies.

People might say that you didn't have enough schooling, that you were born on the wrong side of the tracks, or that you have the wrong last name. They'll use those things to lock you into a season, but you don't have to stay there! Just identify those things and say, "That was only a season!"

Think back to Paul's admonition in Ephesians 5:16 for us to "redeem" the time. That word "redeem" means *to buy up, to rescue from loss,* and *to improve the opportunity.*[6] This means we need to live on purpose and make the most of every situation.

God is able to do exceedingly abundantly above all that we could ever ask or think (Eph. 3:20). The problem is, too often we're not even asking or thinking! We just assume an attitude of "que sera sera" — whatever will be will be.

But our steps are to be ordered by the Lord, so we can't just roll down any old path we want to or accept everything that comes our way. We can't just say, "This is my lot in life, and that's just the way things will be." We have to make the decision, "That it is *not* my lot in life. I am *not* a loser. I am *not* limited!"

You have everything to do with the duration of the seasons you go through, friend. You can extend a good season or shorten a bad one. You can wander in the wilderness for forty years if you want to, or you can just take the ten-day trip.

Bad things will come your way, but you don't have to accept them. Just refuse to grow weary or to stay disappointed. Do the right thing with energy. Determine never to leave a season empty-handed. Work hard. Trust God. And whenever something negative does comes your way, label it with a mental sign that declares, *"This is just a season! I'm moving on to my future and hope in God!"*

---

[6] Strong, "Greek Dictionary of the New Testament," #1805.

2 YOU CAN GET 'UNSTUCK'!

erhaps you are going through an undesirable season right now. If that is the case, I want you to know that it is quite all right for you to desire to come out of that old season so you can enter a more level plain.

We all want greener grass and bluer skies; it's the way God created us. We're always looking for relief because we don't like to suffer. We turn over in bed at night in an unconscious effort to get a little more comfortable. If we get a rock in our shoe, we take off the shoe — even in public — because we want to get that rock out!

We are always pursuing a greater level of peace and comfort. That explains why we want to get out of our undesirable seasons. They don't feel good, and they are certainly *not* a lot of fun!

Our reaction to difficult seasons reminds me of the way my young son once reacted when we put him on a child-sized roller coaster at the county fair. The front car of this little roller coaster was painted to look like a dragon head, and the rest of the cars were painted green. The track on which the roller coaster rode up and down had tiny little hills no more than ten feet high.

But the roller coaster hadn't even gone one lap when our son started screaming. He did *not* want to be on that thing! When I saw the look of panic on my son's face, I walked over to the man operating the ride and asked him if he could stop the roller coaster and let my son get off. The man complied, and I lifted a *very* relieved little boy out of the seat of that tiny roller coaster!

Sometimes in the seasons of life, we hook up on some "rides" that really aren't what we had hoped they would be. When that happens, we feel a lot like my son did on that little roller coaster. We want to scream, "Please stop this ride! I want to get *off*!" We want to get *out* of that season because it isn't fun at all!

The desire to get out of an undesirable season can be the catalyst that brings necessary change to our lives. Whether we find ourselves dealing with sickness, financial reversal, or problems in relationships, there is one thing we're sure of: We *don't* want to camp out and live in the current season!

> The desire
> to get out of
> an undesirable season
> can be the catalyst
> that brings
> necessary change
> to our lives.

So if you are experiencing hard times — whether it be sickness, depression, or any other kind of trouble — consider your desire to enter the next season a good thing. God is a delivering God, and He *wants* to bring you out of trouble, heartache, pain, calamity, adversity, and sorrow. It is His pleasure to bring you into the good future He has always intended for you to enjoy.

That's the main reason you want to get out of that old season anyway — because God never intended for you to go through it in the first place! This knowledge gives you the basis to stand fast on the eternal Word as you pursue a course *out* of the season that has held you back from God's best for far too long.

LOOK TO THE UNSEEN —
THE NEXT SEASON

Many people just decide to live with problems or unresolved conflict in their relationships. There are some family members who haven't spoken in decades! They have assigned the broken relationships to their lives, when the problem should have been assigned to a *season*. Other people have received a diagnosis of sickness and then assigned that sickness to their lives.

But you don't have to live with that bad situation, even if it's of your own making. You don't have to say, "Well, I blew it, so now I'm a loser for life." No, in that season, you may have lost, but there is a new season just around the corner!

Never forget — you do *not* have to accept everything that comes your way. Second Corinthians 4:17,18 tells you what to do instead:

> **For our light affliction, which is but for a moment, is working for us a far more exceeding and eternal weight of glory,**

> **while we do not look at the things which are seen, but at the things which are not seen. For the things which are seen are temporary, but the things which are not seen are eternal.**

The apostle Paul tells you not to look at something in this scripture: You are not to put your focus on *the things which are seen*. Paul is talking here about *your current season*. That means you are to look at what is *not* seen — in other words, your next season and the future seasons beyond.

Some people never stop focusing on their current situation. They spend all their time looking at their mountain of problems and wondering what else will go wrong.

But God says that what is seen — our current season — is temporary. That word "temporary" actually means *for a season, for an occasion,* or *subject to change.*[7] On the other hand, the things that are *not* seen — the future seasons God has planned for us — are eternal. The lessons learned and the blessings enjoyed in those seasons never have to stop; rather, they will continue and be perpetuated into eternity when our time on this earth is through.

We are to look to the season that is ahead of us. Hebrews 11:1 tells us how to do that:

> *We are to look to the season that is ahead of us.*

> **Now faith is the substance of things hoped for, the evidence of things not seen.**

Faith is the spiritual force that reaches into the "things not seen" — the future seasons of life. By contrast, fear keeps us strapped both to this present season and to the old seasons of our past.

---

[7] Ibid., #4340.

Maybe you were once enslaved to some kind of an addiction. If so, don't assign that stronghold to your entire life. Leave it back in that old season. Speak of it as a thing of the past: "I once was addicted to ___." It doesn't matter if you were addicted to drugs, alcohol, pornography, television, or junk food. Whatever you were in bondage to, that bondage belongs in the past. God is calling you now to reach into the unseen by faith!

You see, friend, just because something is unseen doesn't mean it isn't real. It is as real, or even more real, than that which you can see. You just haven't arrived at that season yet.

Consider the example of an apple tree in the springtime. That tree may not have any apples hanging on its branches yet. Nevertheless, resident within the tree lies the unseen potential for enough apples to load that tree down! The apples will come forth in the next season, and the ripe fruit will be harvested from the tree in the season that follows.

By faith, you can look at that tree in the springtime and know that the unseen fruit will surely be ready for harvest in a future season. In the same way, faith pulls you out of the old season by looking to the unseen — the future blessings of God to be manifested in a season yet to come.

CRY OUT TO THE LORD

Let me share one of the major keys to your deliverance from an undesirable season. The principle is really very simple, and it is found in Psalm 34:4:

I sought the Lord, and He heard me, and delivered me from all my fears.

45

This same message is repeated throughout the Scriptures. God is the Deliverer. He is the One who can help you. He is the One who can rescue you. Therefore, you need to decide on the inside once and for all where your help comes from.

Who can help us? Certainly our help doesn't come from Oprah or Maury. Nor does it come from the government, our mama, or our neighbor. Our help doesn't come from the luck of the draw, the lottery, or any other earthly source. Our help comes *only* from the Lord who made heaven and earth (Ps. 121:1,2)!

If you cry out to God, He obligates Himself to hear you and to act on your behalf. So if you're in a situation you don't like, don't let that situation remain the way it is — call out to God! Sometimes He'll correct you. Sometimes He'll adjust things. But no matter how He answers your prayer, the end result will be deliverance!

I once asked the Lord, "Why is it so important that we call out to You? Why does it bring such a powerful response?"

> ...If you're in a situation you don't like, don't let that situation remain the way it is — call out to God!

This is the answer the Holy Spirit spoke to my heart: *"Because I want to hear from you. I want to hear you say, 'I need Your help, Lord.'"*

Something happens when you choose not to keep quiet during the stormy times of life, but instead you choose to declare, "God, I want You to help me." When God hears you cry out to Him for help, He immediately goes into action.

46

Why? Because that's all God has been waiting to hear. From the start to the end of the Bible, His message is always the same: He wants you to have no other gods before you. He doesn't want either you or anyone else to try to fix your life. You or others may have a part to play, but, ultimately, your cry must go out to Him.

Where do you want to go, friend? What do you want to be? Whatever dreams God has placed within your heart for the future, you will only enter the season that lies up ahead by first depending on Him for the help you need to get out of the *present* season.

Don't just say, "This is my life, and it's a big mess!" The Bible says that God will make your crooked places straight (Isa. 40:4). He will make your rough places smooth. He will fill in your valleys and bring your high places down low so you can walk on a level plain. Even if you have to climb mountains and make your way through rugged crags and cliffs, God promises to give you hinds' feet for the high places and sure footing on even the most treacherous of paths (Hab. 3:19).

More times than I could ever count, I have prayed, "Lord, I want You to help me. I don't know what to do in this situation, and I don't know how to do it. I don't have anyone to turn to except You." And every time I have cried unto the Lord, He has heard me and delivered me out of all my troubles — just as He will do for you.

'You Have Dwelt Here Long Enough'

In Deuteronomy 1, the children of Israel are reminded of a profound message they had received from the Lord — a message that applies just as much to us today as it did to the Israelites so many years ago. In effect, God told His people, "You've been here long enough; it's time to move on."

> **"...You have dwelt long enough at this mountain.**
> **"Turn and take your journey, and go to the mountains of the Amorites, to all the neighboring places in the plain, in the mountains and in the lowland, in the South and on the seacoast, to the land of the Canaanites and to Lebanon, as far as the great river, the River Euphrates.**
> **"See, I have set the land before you; go in and possess the land which the Lord swore to your fathers — to Abraham, Isaac, and Jacob — to give to them and their descendants after them."**
>
> Deuteronomy 1:6-8

God first gave the Israelites that message at a place called Horeb. That Hebrew word for "Horeb" actually means *the burnt or parched region.*[8] Obviously, this was *not* a desirable place to camp out at for a long period of time!

First God told the people that they had stayed too long in the burnt and parched region. Then He gave them a command: He told them to march straight into Canaan, the Promised Land, and take it for themselves. Canaan was theirs, for He had already promised to give it to them. However, the Israelites still had some things *they* had to do: They had to *get up; march away* from that mountain where they had been stuck for too long; *enter* the Promised Land; and, finally, *possess* the land for themselves.

Have you been staying too long at "Horeb"? If so, God is saying to you, "You've been there long enough. You need to get out of that old season." Where are you supposed to

---

[8] Strong, "Hebrew Dictionary of the Old Testament," #2717.

go? He wants you to march straight into your promised land with no more delays and no more detours. The burnt and parched region you've been traveling is *not* your life. It is just a season!

Canaan was a type of our land of promise, where we enjoy the abundant life God has always intended for us to enjoy while we live on this earth. Canaan is where our future is. That's where we'll find better days, so that's where we are headed. We're leaving the burnt and parched places where we've lingered for too long, and we're going to a better place!

> The burnt and parched region you've been traveling is *not* your life. It is just a season!

This isn't some "pie-in-the-sky" message that tells us what we can expect when we all get to Heaven. I'm talking about our "steak-on-the-plate" life here on this earth!

Don't Cope — Get Delivered!

Remember — I'm not saying that everything will always go our way or that we won't have any problems in this life. There will always be challenges to face as long as we walk on this earth. But if we're not careful, we'll get stuck in the season where we first encountered a problem, trying to cope with the problem instead of overcoming it and moving on.

Whether we experience difficulties in a relationship, receive a bad doctor's report, or get laid off in the midst of a shaky economy, we're often tempted to just slide over and share our bed with the problems we face. We cope with this problem and resign ourselves to that problem; we carry this burden and live with that burden. Soon we find ourselves stuck in Horeb, going around the same mountain again and again and again.

But the truth is, believers don't cope well because they were never designed to cope. Believers are supposed to be delivered!

> ...Believers don't cope well because they were never designed to cope. Believers are supposed to be delivered!

You're not to cope with the undesirable seasons of your life — you can be delivered from them! The devil will come to you pretending to be a game show host and declare, "This problem is your life!" But you need to come right back at him with an answer born of faith: "No, you dirty dog, *this is just a season!*"

Don't cope with symptoms of sickness or adverse circumstances — *get delivered.* You have a Savior who came to rescue you and help you. You've been in Horeb long enough. Now it's time for you to move on out and head toward your promised land!

ASSIGN THOSE NEGATIVE THINGS TO A SEASON!

But to start that process, you first have to make some determinations about the seasons of your life. You have to ask yourself:

- *Do I want to stay in the season I'm in right now?*
- *Are there things I want to get rid of or change?*
- *Are there things in this season I want to keep forever?*

Answering those questions will help you determine what to assign to your life and what to assign only to that particular season.

I remember the time Alicia and I ministered these principles to a woman from our congregation who lay in intensive care, having suffered from a long-term bout with sickness. I told this woman, "Just because you've been fighting this sickness for a long time, you shouldn't accept it as your life. You have to start seeing this as a season."

Then I asked the woman what she wanted to do after she was healed. "How many children did you want to have? Where do you want to go? What do you want to be?"

I did my best that day to get her eyes off her symptoms and to jump-start her faith. I wanted to help her get unstuck from that season of sickness so she could begin reaching by faith into the next season where God's blessings awaited her.

If you've been dragging trash from your old seasons into new seasons, you've been doing it long enough. It's time to get rid of those hindrances. It's time to move on.

If you were made fun of or abused as a child, assign that to your childhood. Don't carry that baggage around your entire life, always dwelling on the negative things that your daddy or mama or coach or teacher said. Yes, you may have experienced hurts, disappointments, and failures. But you can assign all those negative things to a season and move on into your future and your hope!

As another example, let's apply this principle to the area of business and finances. Maybe you had a failed business venture or made some bad decisions that put your family finances in jeopardy. Perhaps you lost one, two, or even three jobs.

What do you do in this type of situation? Don't allow yourself to think that you won't be able to get or keep a job for the rest of your life. Don't allow yourself to think that you're no good or that you'll never get promoted. Assign these failures to a season, not to the rest of your life. Then as quickly as you can, get away from that season!

This same principle applies to our relationships, our health, and every other area of our lives. *We CAN get out of undesirable seasons by trusting in the absolute truth of God's Word.*

You may be in a dead-end situation. It may look like such a mess that there seems to be no way out. But Jesus, the Anointed One, came to redeem you from that mess, to rescue you from loss, and to improve your opportunity.

There *is* a way out, and there are better days ahead! You may be in a mess right now, but don't assign it to your whole life. Limit it, label it, and call it a *season*!

FIND AND PURSUE GOD'S WILL

Here is another key to getting unstuck from an undesirable season: You must first *find* and then *pursue* God's will for you. I'm talking about seeking to discover God's plans, thoughts, and intentions for your life, for that *is* His will. Once you find that out, your next step is to pursue His will with all your heart, mind, soul, and strength.

It is important in this process that you maintain an honest heart at all times. If you don't have an honest heart, you'll either ignore the Word of God, or you'll twist the Word to fit your purpose. You'll also play the blame game — and in the blame game, you never win any prizes, even if you're only blaming the devil.

This is an extremely important point to heed on your way out of a difficult season. *Don't play the blame game.* Instead, entrust yourself to God, for He alone is the One who keeps the books. If you want to get out of that season you're in right now, you must have an honest heart and stop blaming everyone else for your problems.

Some people want to get out of a situation, but they don't have a scriptural basis to get out. They'll vacillate all over the place trying to decide what course to take because they don't have an honest heart. They're not willing to obey God's will, no matter what He tells them to do.

One moment these people will tell you that the Lord is telling them to go a certain direction. But three weeks later, you'll see them take a different course. If you say to them, "I thought God was telling you to go that other direction," they'll answer, "Well, yes, but now He's telling me to do this." What a fickle god they serve!

But our God is the same yesterday, today, and forever (Heb. 13:8). He doesn't change His mind after He has told us which direction to take. That's why we have to come before God with an honest heart to determine His will for our lives. If we don't, we will cater to our flesh and emotions, leaving ourselves wide open and vulnerable to deception.

Break Every Wrong Perception

As you seek God's will, you must also determine to break any wrong views you hold of yourself.

A lot of people have a very bad view of themselves because the devil has been working on them since the day they were born. Maybe they were always the last ones to be picked to play on teams during school recess. As they grew to adulthood, perhaps they were overlooked again and again when it came time for promotion or reward. As a result, these people often live their lives feeling unworthy and unforgiven, even after they become Christians.

The enemy has probably worked overtime in your life as well to ruin your perception of yourself and of how God views you. That's why it's up to you to change or correct any perception you hold that doesn't line up with God's Word. You do that by grabbing hold of two central truths: 1) *God is faithful*, and 2) *His Word is true and will work for you.*

> ...It's up to you to change or correct any perception you hold that doesn't line up with God's Word.

So use the truth in God's Word to break any wrong view or perception of yourself or of your circumstances. Realize that according to the power in God's Word, your situation can change. Start declaring by faith that there *is* a way out!

Jesus had something to say about this subject of perception in Matthew 6:22,23:

"The lamp of the body is the eye. If therefore your eye is good, your whole body will be full of light.

"But if your eye is bad, your whole body will be full of darkness. If therefore the light that is in you is darkness, how great is that darkness!"

What do you do with your eyes? You *see* with them. Therefore, the figurative analogy we would draw from Jesus' words here is that our eye is our *view* or our *perception*. If we perceive things correctly, our lives will be filled with the light of God's Presence and blessing. But if we have a cloudy, unhealthy view of ourselves and our surrounding circumstances, our lives will be filled with darkness.

I'm a loser. I can't ever get ahead. Nothing ever goes right for me. People don't even notice me when I walk past. Do those kinds of negative thoughts fill your mind on a regular basis? If so, the darkness of those wrong thoughts will begin to fill your life. On the other hand, if you purpose to see things clearly according to what God says in His Word, your life will begin to be filled with the light of His truth.

You see, God is not a respecter of *persons*; He is a respecter of *principles*. We can see this truth borne out in the story of Cain and Abel in Genesis 4. God respected Abel and his offering but did *not* respect Cain and his offering. However, the difference in His response to the two men's offerings was a matter of *principle*, not of *personalities*. It was what Abel brought as an offering and how he brought it that caused God to respect him. In contrast, it was what Cain brought to the Lord and how he brought it that caused God *not* to respect him.

Thus, if you do what Abel did, you can have what Abel had, for God never ceases to respect His eternal principles. It's just a matter of doing things the way God wants them done, for He always honors obedience.

God is faithful. His Word is true. His promises will work for you. You have to believe those basic premises right up front, or you will continue to remain stuck in Horeb — in the burnt, parched regions of defeat and frustration.

You have to tell yourself, "I believe that God is faithful above everything else. Maybe I haven't gotten His Word to fully work in my life yet; nevertheless, His Word is still true. I'm not going to put any blame or limitations on God. If anything, I'll blame myself. But I'm learning and growing. I'm getting a clearer view of my life every day. And I know that God's Word *will* work for me to get me out of this old season and into the good future He has planned for me!"

MOVING OUT OF A SEASON
STEP BY STEP

Coming out of a season is usually progressive, with deliverance coming in stages rather than all at once. Thank God, there *are* times that He immediately snatches us out of the pit in which we've become mired. We all like those times of quick deliverance! But more often than not, we come out of an old season step by step.

Many times Christians don't understand this principle. They say, "Well, I prayed and I believed God all afternoon, and I'm still in the same situation." But are they really in the same situation — or are they *coming out of* that situation?

Once again, let me emphasize: *Our perception about our situation is crucial in determining the outcome.* Are we stuck in our current season, or are we coming out of it? We need to continually keep in mind what God said: "You've been there long enough. Now it's time to get up and head out toward the land of promise. Go in and possess it!"

As you take steps to come out of the undesirable season you're in right now, here's something else for you to understand: Sometimes the longer you've been in a season, the longer it takes to get out of it — or more accurately, the longer it takes for the season to get out of *you*.

Consider the example of the Israelites. They spent 430 years in slavery and bondage to Egypt before they were set free. Finally, the Lord delivered them, and they entered into a new season. However, from the way the children of Israel rebelled after their deliverance, it is obvious that they still had bondage and slavery living on the inside of them. God Himself wasn't successful in getting the old season of bondage out of that older generation. As a result, they had to die in the wilderness.

Only Joshua and Caleb shook off the old season and held fast in faith to God's promise for a better future. Of that older generation, only Joshua and Caleb ever made it into the Promised Land. That bondage mentality had to die off completely before the younger generation could go in to possess the land.

GO FOR THE ROOT
OF THE PROBLEM!

This confirms the principle we've been discussing: *We have to somehow kill the wrong perception that says we will forever be trapped in the current season.* The only way we can accomplish this is to go after the root of the problem that is binding us to that old season. But to do that, we must first grasp this principle: *What we feed grows, and what we starve dies.*

The reason certain wrong perceptions or sins remain strong in our lives is that we feed them. We can only kill those negative perceptions and sinful strongholds as we 1) *refuse to feed them* and 2) *attack the roots.* The result of such a strategy is described in Job 18:16: *"His roots are dried out below, and his branch withers above."*

Isaiah 5 speaks to this principle of attacking the root of a problem that has hindered us and caused disappointment in our lives.

> **My Well-beloved has a vineyard on a very fruitful hill.**
> **He dug it up and cleared out its stones, and planted it with the choicest vine. He built a tower in its midst, and also made a winepress in it; so He expected it to bring forth good grapes, but it brought forth wild grapes.**
> **"And now, O inhabitants of Jerusalem and men of Judah, judge, please, between Me and My vineyard.**
> **"What more could have been done to My vineyard that I have not done in it? Why then, when I expected it to bring forth good grapes, did it bring forth wild grapes?"**
>
> **Isaiah 5:1-4**

Have you ever had something like that happen in your life? In other words, have you ever worked hard at something and therefore expected a good result, only to reap a harvest of nothing but poisonous, bitter berries? It reminds me of some of my amateur gardening experiences. Sometimes I plant seed in expectation of a wonderful, abundant harvest. I carefully fertilize, water, and weed my garden — only to reap mutated fruit and vegetables that end up being thrown over the fence.

You have to realize that sometimes disappointment comes into your life even after you have worked hard to achieve a goal. Notice in verse 1 that this vineyard was planted on a very fruitful hill. In the same way, there are times that you try hard to invest your energy, effort, and time into the right endeavor. Yet despite all your hard work, the expected harvest just doesn't happen and things don't go well for you.

In that case, what are you to do? Let's read on:

> **"And now, please let Me tell you what I will do to My vineyard: I will take away its hedge, and it shall be burned; and break down its wall, and it shall be trampled down.**
> **"I will lay it waste; it shall not be pruned or dug, but there shall come up briers and thorns. I will also command the clouds that they rain no rain on it."**
>
> Isaiah 5:5,6

Do you know what God is saying in this passage of Scripture? If you put a great deal of effort into an endeavor and it doesn't work out right, *you need to stop nurturing it.* You don't keep putting quarters in an out-of-order Coke machine!

We're talking about a season of your life here. Maybe you stepped out to do something that you thought was the right thing to do. You worked hard to reach the intended goal, but in the end, it didn't turn out the way you wanted it to. In that case, you need to understand that you shouldn't nurture that dream anymore. If some goal you have pursued is producing only bitter, poisonous berries in your life, *don't nurture that dream any longer*. Wise up, and stop protecting a bad harvest!

In Matthew 15:13, Jesus says, *"...Every plant which My heavenly Father has not planted will be uprooted."* So here is the principle you have to get hold of: *What was not planted by the Father — what He never intended for you in the first place — CAN be uprooted!*

Sometimes Christians say, "This addiction, this bondage, has been in my family for three to four generations."

But if it isn't what God intended, it can be uprooted.

"Yes, but that's just the way we are."

Well, then, determine to change the way you are!

"But that's the way my whole family is!"

Then find a new family. Come into the family of God!

You see, friend, sooner or later you'll have to deal with the problems that have kept you stuck in an old season. Sooner or later, you'll have to attack the roots. When you do, take comfort in what you've just learned: *If the Father didn't plant it, it CAN be uprooted.*

> *What was not planted by the Father — what He never intended for you in the first place — CAN be uprooted!*

ATTACK THE ROOTS
WITH THE SWORD OF THE WORD

How do you go about attacking the root of your problem? Jesus tells you what to do in Matthew 3:10:

And even now the ax is laid to the root of the trees. Therefore every tree which does not bear good fruit is cut down and thrown into the fire.

Is there something you don't want in your life, such as sickness, financial debt, unforgiveness, anger, depression, a wrong attitude, or a sinful habit? Do you have the scriptural foundation to declare that it isn't what the Father intended for you? Well, whether the problem lies in your relationships, your health, your finances, or any other area of your life — you need to lay the ax to the root. Destroy the root of the vine that is producing the bitter fruit in your life!

What is that ax? The Word of God. In fact, the Word is likened to not only an ax in the Bible, but to fire, to a sword, and to a hammer as well. And any one of those things can be used as a weapon to attack those poisonous roots!

The priority here is to destroy the root of the problem that is producing bad fruit in your life. Cut it, beat it, stomp on it, spit on it, burn it — do whatever you have to do. Your only other alternative is to accept the current season as your lot in life — and that just isn't true! It is only a season, and you've been there long enough!

That's what you have to determine on the inside of you once and for all. You have to lock down on that truth deep on the inside of you. Locate it; get it in your crosshairs; punch in the coordinates; and fire off your declaration of faith: "I have been here long enough. I am *not* sitting still and allowing this problem to defeat me any longer!" Then go after the root and whack it with the sword of God's Word!

But understand this: The Word of God becomes a sword *when you put it in your mouth* — not when you cross-stitch it or silently read your little breadbox promise of the day. You have to *speak forth* the Word, declaring in faith:

"Old things have passed away, and all things have become new in my life. My God will supply all my needs according to His riches in glory. The Lord will perfect that which concerns me. I can do *all* things through Christ who strengthens me. When I cry out to God, He hears and delivers me. I'm surrounded with favor as with a shield. By Jesus' stripes I am healed. The same Spirit who raised Jesus from the dead dwells in me, quickens me, and makes me strong!"

At the church where I pastor, we're continually confessing, "I am what the Word of God says I am. I have what the Word of God says I have. I can do what it says I can do." That's a great confession to make, but we can't stop there. We have to get in the Word and *find out* who we are, what we have, and what we can do in Christ; then we have to put those powerful truths in our mouths and declare them over our situation by faith. As we do that, the Word becomes a mighty sword that begins to destroy the problem we face at its very roots.

Don't try to cope with your current season — start *talking* to it! Tell it that you've been here long enough. Don't allow yourself to settle back into complacency after reading this book, saying, "Well, the author said some things that make sense, but, in reality, this is my life." It's only your life if you want it to be!

PURSUE A FUTURE
THAT SHINES EVER BRIGHTER

So what does God have to say about the manner in which we are to come out of our undesirable seasons? Isaiah 55:12 tells us:

> **"For you shall go out with joy, and be led out with peace; the mountains and the hills shall break forth into singing before you, and all the trees of the field shall clap their hands."**

How should you go out? *With joy!* When you come out of your difficult situation, you should be grinning, dancing, and shouting, "That problem held me in a headlock for such a long time — *but now I'm free!*"

Let's read on, for verse 13 has something important to tell us as well:

> **"Instead of the thorn shall come up the cypress tree, and instead of the brier shall come up the myrtle tree; and it shall be to the Lord for a name, for an everlasting sign that shall not be cut off."**

The thorn is figurative of *cursing* and *mockery*; we can see this in the case of the crown of thorns placed on Jesus' head. The thorn can also signify *to bind* or *to hinder*. Thus, this scripture is saying that the thorny problems that have bound and hindered you in the previous season will be replaced by the cypress tree in the new season.

The cypress tree symbolizes the concepts of *rich deposits, strength, fragrant,* and *not being susceptible to rot or to becoming worm-eaten*. Similarly, instead of briers — which also signify *curse* and *stinging torment* — shall grow the myrtle tree. The myrtle tree is a beautiful evergreen, used for perfume and seasonings, and symbolic of *peace* and *joy*.

This reminds us that God is thinking, planning, and intending for us to enjoy a future of peace and not of evil (Jer. 29:11). Psalm 34:14 has something further to say about this subject: *"Depart from evil and do good; seek peace and pursue it."*

Traditionally, we read this verse as follows: "Stop doing wrong, and begin to do the right thing. Seek peace — get along with folks — and put some effort behind it." Now, certainly this interpretation is accurate and applies to our lives. But I want to look at this scripture in light of our discussion on seasons, highlighting the same Hebrew words, translated *peace* and *evil*, that we found in Jeremiah 29:11.

Let's look at Psalm 34:14 again, keeping in mind the definitions for "peace" and "evil" we discussed earlier. First, it says, "Depart from evil — from adversity, affliction, misery, sorrow, and calamity." In other words, God is saying, "You're free to go. You don't have to stay in that undesirable season any longer. Change *can* come; you *can* depart from the evil circumstances of the past."

The verse goes on to say, "Do good; seek peace and pursue it." God is saying, "You're free to begin to behave wisely. Seek peace — seek to be happy and well and whole. But don't only seek peace — *pursue* it. Go after it with all your strength!"

You need to find out what God intends for you — His plan of peace for your life — and then you need to pursue it. You've been at this place long enough. It's time to get up and get moving. It's time to march yourself straight into your personal promised land so you can finally possess what has belonged to you all along.

It all starts with a determination on the inside that says, "I'm coming out of this situation and circumstance. I'm not going to be held by it any longer!" You do *major* damage to the root of your problem just by making that declaration of faith.

You are called to go from faith to faith, from strength to strength, from victory to victory, from glory to glory (2 Cor. 3:18). You're called to go from where you are to a better place, for as the Bible says, the path of the just shines ever brighter until the perfect day (Prov. 4:18)!

> It's time to march yourself straight into your personal promised land so you can finally possess what has belonged to you all along.

For those of us who are Christians, life is never supposed to be about going down in defeat. Life in God is about seeing His hand move on our behalf to bring victory, no matter what's going on around us. Although ten thousand fall at our right hand, God will uphold us, protect us, and lead us out of evil to His good plan on the other side!

So go ahead and get that truth planted deep in your heart. Use the sword of the Word to slice through every obstacle as you declare in faith:

"I'm *not* going down. I'm not in this life to decrease. I'm not living on this earth just to get worn out so that I can barely float up to shore. I'm not only going to make it to the end of my spiritual race — I'm going to look great when I get there, because my path is shining brighter day by day!"

WISDOM: THE KEY TO DELIVERANCE

3

*W*hen I was growing up, my family bought our tennis shoes at discount department stores. I don't think I ever owned a pair of real leather dress shoes. My dress shoes just *looked* like they were made of leather — until I scuffed them. There was no hiding those scuff marks!

Soon after Alicia and I started the church we now pastor, a couple in the church came to me and said they wanted to bless me with some shoes. They instructed me to go to a certain upscale department store and to order a pair of shoes. I gladly accepted the couple's generous offer and went to the designated store to order my new shoes.

However, when I told the salesman behind the counter which shoes I wanted to order, the man said, "I can't let you order those shoes."

I thought, *I must be over the price limit.*

Then the man said, "They want you to buy any shoes you'd like, but nothing under this dollar amount."

So I ordered a different, more expensive pair of shoes. Then the man told me, "There is one other thing you need to do before you leave. The couple told me not to tell you this until after you had ordered the first pair of shoes: You're supposed to order a second pair as well, and they are also not to be under this dollar amount." Feeling very blessed, I ordered my second pair of shoes.

After the man sized my feet, I ordered the size I thought I needed. When the shoes arrived, I was elated. At that point in my life, they were the finest shoes I'd ever had in my life! But there was an unexpected problem: The shoes were way too tight.

Did I take the shoes back? No, I didn't want to hurt the feelings of the couple who bought them for me. So I wore those expensive shoes, and I even preached in them. But even though they were high-quality shoes, they were killing me! After the church service, I'd go back to my office and pull off the shoes. I'd rub my feet; I'd pray for my feet. Then I'd put the shoes back on to preach another service.

I had toe surgery twice because of those shoes. They were simply too small for me, yet I continued to put up with them. However, I'll tell you something — today I'm the most finicky and skilled shoe shopper you will ever meet! Why? Because I know what it is to wear shoes that are too tight, and I'm *not* going back there! If I find some shoes I really like, I'll try them on. But if they're too tight, I don't buy them, no matter how much I like them. I've learned my lesson about tolerating shoes that are too cramped for comfort!

The Place Where You Dwell
Is Too Small

There are places in our lives that are just like those shoes. I'm talking about those undesirable seasons where everything feels too cramped, too crowded, too tight and uncomfortable. When we're in a season like that, the pressure seems continual, and it's the last place we want to stay.

Although we all have a million different reasons to explain why we feel that way, the solution is the same for every one of us: *God is the One who delivers us out of trouble.* That word "trouble" actually carries the meaning of *a narrow, tight, cramped space* — a place we want to get out of so we can enter the wide open, free place that God has laid out before us.

Sometimes we act like I did with those expensive, uncomfortable shoes. We think we have too much invested in the current season to move on — but meanwhile, we're miserable!

Listen, it's time for change, friend. It's time to get out of that tight place and move on. It's time for something supernatural to happen in your life!

Second Kings 6 tells us about an incident in the prophet Elisha's ministry that wonderfully symbolizes this exact message:

> And the sons of the prophets said to Elisha, "See now, the place where we dwell with you is too small for us.
> "Please, let us go to the Jordan, and let every man take a beam from there, and let us make there a place where we may dwell." So he answered, "Go."

Then one said, "Please consent to go with your servants." And he answered, "I will go."

So he went with them. And when they came to the Jordan, they cut down trees.

But as one was cutting down a tree, the iron ax head fell into the water; and he cried out and said, "Alas, master! For it was borrowed."

So the man of God said, "Where did it fall?" And he showed him the place. So he cut off a stick, and threw it in there; and he made the iron float.

2 Kings 6:1-6

First of all, I want you to notice what the sons of the prophets said to Elisha: "The place where we dwell is too small." They were talking about a physical dwelling place, but the same principle applies to the spiritual realm. We need to come to the place where we realize, "I've been here long enough. This place is too tight and cramped for me."

> We need to come to the place where we realize, "I've been here long enough. This place is too tight and cramped for me."

That's when we should reach out by faith for God's supernatural power to help us move on. We've been at that place long enough. It's time to move on to that free, open place up ahead of us!

Let's look a little more closely at what this passage of Scripture is telling us along this line. In verse 5, a son of a prophet is whacking on a tree with an ax when suddenly the ax head flies off and lands in the nearby water. It then does what any iron ax head would do — it sinks!

The man immediately calls out to the prophet Elisha for help in retrieving the ax head. Elisha asks where it fell. After being shown the spot, the prophet cuts off a stick and throws it in the water. Suddenly the iron ax head reappears and floats on the water!

That is a miracle, friend. Something like that just doesn't happen in the natural. You could go out to a nearby pond this afternoon and throw sticks in it all you want, but nothing is going to come floating up to the water surface — especially not something made out of iron! This was a supernatural occurrence that helped the sons of the prophets get out of their dwelling place that had become too small.

God supplies many supernatural things in all our lives, and He does it much more often than we realize. So often He moves on our behalf supernaturally and we don't even notice. Why? Because we weren't really expecting Him to come through for us!

If we want God's supernatural power demonstrated in our lives, we'll have to change our expectation. We need to wipe the dust of neglect off our spiritual windshield and say, "I'm *expecting* God to act. I'm on the constant lookout for certain things to happen. I'm expecting 'super' on my 'natural'!"

YOU HAVE A PART TO PLAY

Now let's look at what Elisha said next to the man who lost the ax head:

> **Therefore he said, "Pick it up for yourself." So he reached out his hand and took it.**
>
> **2 Kings 6:7**

71

Even with supernatural help, you still have a part to play in determining the outcome of your situation. Yes, God brings His supernatural power on the scene and causes ax heads to float. But when that happens, you aren't supposed to sit back and build a tabernacle to commemorate the event. Or you don't say, "Wow! I'm going to take a picture of this and send it to So-and-so so he can use it in his ministry newsletter!"

The prophet told the younger man, "Reach out and pick up the ax head for yourself." God's supernatural power does move on our behalf, but then *we* have to do something. We have to *reach out* by faith and *receive* the miracle!

There is something else in this passage that confirms the importance of doing our part. Notice what the sons of the prophets did after telling Elisha, "The place where we dwell is too small." Did they pass around a petition? Did they sit around their little card table and do nothing but gripe and complain? No, they didn't. They said, "Give us permission to go out and cut down some beams. We're going to build us a bigger place!"

Instead of sitting around and complaining that their dwelling place was too tight and small, the sons of the prophets got active and did something. I believe the Spirit of God is calling His people to do the same: "Get up and start doing what you have to do to build a better future. And as you expect My power to move on your behalf, the supernatural *will* come!"

I'm sure you could use some of God's supernatural power in your life right now. Maybe you need "an ax head to float" in certain areas of your life, such as your health, your children, your marriage, or your finances. Maybe you've been working on something God has called you to do in ministry or business, but you're still thinking too small.

Whatever your situation, it's time to come out of that cramped space. You have to "pick up the ax head" and decide, "I'm coming out of this. This place has gotten too small. It doesn't fit me well at all anymore!"

Then you need to realize that although the Holy Spirit is your Helper, *you* are the doer. You may be saying, "I wish God would help me by giving me a miracle." Meanwhile, God could be trying to get this message across to you: "I'm still waiting for you to do *your* part!"

"But I *can't* do it," you may protest. Correction — you can't do it without God's help. But if you'll step out by faith to do what God has called you to do, the strength and supernatural ability of the Helper will immediately be present to help you.

Too often we place blame on others as an excuse for not stepping out in faith and moving toward the future and hope God has for us. We say we're waiting on someone else to act, or we're waiting for all the conditions to be favorable before we do anything.

But I have news for you — on this side of eternity, conditions will never be perfect. You just have to step out and do what you know to do.

You may say, "Well, I'm afraid." I like what Joyce Meyer says about that: "Do it afraid." In other words, you know what to do, so just step out there and do it, and act as if you're *not* afraid!

You see, the devil is trying to scare you, lie to you, and discourage you. He wants you to be fearful and timid. Therefore, I believe the number-one way to resist the enemy, outside of using the sword of the Word, is to ignore him. You'll frustrate the devil so much that you'll ruin his lunch! Meanwhile, you'll be getting yourself in position to see God's supernatural power demonstrated on your behalf!

Above All, Get Wisdom

Even with supernatural help, you must pick up the miracle for yourself on your way out of an undesirable season. You can't do God's part, and God won't do your part.

You'll find another important key that is yours to pick up and apply to your life in Proverbs 4:5-7:

> **Get wisdom! Get understanding! Do not forget, nor turn away from the words of my mouth.**
> **Do not forsake her, and she will preserve you; love her, and she will keep you.**
> **Wisdom is the principal thing; therefore get wisdom.**

Get wisdom. This principle is a key in preserving, maintaining, and increasing God's blessings in your life. You can only reach that goal by going after the supernatural kind of wisdom that comes from above.

The extent to which you obey God's command to pursue wisdom will determine your vantage point as you go through the seasons of life. The higher the wisdom you obtain, the better vantage point you will have and the more clearly you'll be able to see how to negotiate yourself through the complicated maze of every difficult situation.

Divine wisdom is one of the "ax heads" that God causes to float; then He expects us to go after it and pick it up. Contrary to what we might desire, wisdom is *not* going to automatically come to us. We're not going to just wake up one morning and suddenly be all-wise! No, gaining wisdom is a process and requires diligent effort on our part. However, as children of God, we can rejoice in knowing that we have continual access to a supernatural Source of infinite wisdom, the Holy Spirit Himself.

> The extent to which you obey God's command to pursue wisdom will determine your vantage point as you go through the seasons of life.

In the meantime, you and I need to make it our goal to behave wisely in the affairs of life. But we don't have to figure things out for ourselves. We can ask God, who promised to give wisdom liberally to anyone who asks for it (James 1:5).

All of us have watched people react foolishly when suddenly faced with a problem. We've also seen people who respond admirably and with wisdom when a difficult challenge arises. Why are we able to differentiate between an individual who is acting wisely and someone else who is acting unwisely? Because God has made wisdom available to us. The Bible actually says that wisdom *cries out* (Prov. 8:1-3). In other words, if we'll get quiet in our hearts and listen, we'll have a hard time missing what God has to say about behaving wisely in every situation of life.

THE BENEFITS OF BEHAVING WISELY

First Samuel 18:14 says that David behaved wisely in all his ways. In the Hebrew, that phrase "behaved wisely" in part means *prospered and was successful*.[9] Thus, we can conclude that those who behave wisely will prosper and be successful. On the other hand, people who continually make foolish choices are *not* going to end up on the side of prosperity and success!

David received some benefits because he behaved himself wisely. These are the same benefits *you* will need in your life in order to get out of an old season and into a new one. Let's look at the benefits David enjoyed as mentioned in this passage of Scripture.

First, David received *promotion* (v. 13). Now, don't limit this principle merely to promotion at your workplace or an increase in your checkbook balance. Spread its powerful truth over your entire life, and remember — promotion ultimately comes from the Lord.

If you're like most folks, you'd like to experience promotion in your life. But for that to come to pass, you will have to behave wisely. For instance, if you "cut the fool" at your job by being unreliable or acting disrespectfully toward your superiors, there won't be promotion in your next season — unless, of course, the boss is your overindulgent mama!

The second benefit David received was *favor* (v. 16). We all need favor in our lives. Favor causes doors of opportunity

---

[9] Ibid., #7919.

to open and doors of disappointment and defeat to be shut in our lives — and this passage tells us that we obtain favor by behaving wisely in every area of life. Then we can *expect* favor to overtake us as we declare in faith over ourselves, "I am a favor magnet!"

The Bible says that favor surrounds you like a shield, so start looking for it every time you walk into a new situation. Don't be surprised at anything. Just keep a lookout for the favor of God, and as you behave wisely, you will find it!

The Bible also says that because David behaved wisely, *the Lord was with him* (v. 14). You may say, "That's no big deal. The Lord is with me too." But this phrase "the Lord was with him" is remarkable. It actually refers to an intimacy with God that is on an entirely different level than most Christians enjoy. And just as the Lord was with David, He will also be with you as you learn to behave yourself wisely in every situation of life.

Another result of David's choice to behave wisely was that his enemies were afraid of him (v. 15). This word "afraid" means *to turn aside and shrink in fear*.[10] David's enemies were afraid of him because they could see time and time again that the Lord was David's Deliverer.

Proverbs 28:26 says, *"He who trusts in his own heart is a fool, but whoever walks wisely will be delivered."* I like that word "delivered." It means *to be smooth* or *to escape as if by slipperiness*.[11] It can also carry the meaning *to emit sparks*.[11] Put all these concepts together, and the word "delivered" means this: If you will behave wisely when you're in a tight situation,

---

[10] Ibid., #1481.

[11] Ibid., #4422.

you will slide right out of that mess — and on your way out, you can emit some sparks. I like the sound of that!

The children of Israel enjoyed this benefit as well as they went about obeying God's command to possess the land of Canaan. One of the cities they were commanded to take was the city of Jericho, a well-fortified city with thick walls and a large army. In a worldly sense, the people of Jericho were secure; but then this nomad bunch called the Israelites came along, who hardly had a weapon to their name!

The woman Rahab told the two Israelite spies that the people were afraid of Israel. Why? *Because they knew that the Lord was with the children of Israel* (Joshua 2:11). They had heard of Israel's victories against other Canaanite cities, and their hearts melted as they wondered what was going to happen to them.

You'll begin to carry yourself a little differently once you understand that your enemies are afraid of you — especially your greatest enemy, the devil! I'm not saying you'll go right out and buy a Superfly hat, but you *will* perk up and walk through this life with more confidence as you learn to behave wisely in all the affairs of life.

You Have To *Continue* in Wisdom

Now, here is another important point: Don't behave wisely just long enough to get out of your current season. If you get into the next season and start acting unwisely, you will end up in problems all over again. That's why some people are on their fifth marriage, their forty-eighth job, or their sixty-third diet. It's also the reason many of them are paying off their MasterCard with their Visa!

We have to have wisdom to get out of undesirable seasons, and we have to continue to operate in wisdom to *stay* free. Otherwise, we'll end up cycling back through another rough situation all over again.

The person who stops behaving wisely is very prone to repeat the same mistakes in his next season. However, every time he recycles through certain negative events in his life, he never finds it the same as the last time; rather, the situation is always worse.

> We have to have wisdom to get out of undesirable seasons, and we have to continue to operate in wisdom to *stay* free.

One of the more difficult aspects of ministry is watching people get themselves into a bind over and over again. In the beginning, I have the joy of helping them call on God for deliverance. I give them instruction in the Word, pray with them, and encourage them to make some good decisions, such as getting more involved in church and changing the kind of people they hang around with. But many times when the pressure is off, these same people will go right back to where they were again.

I've seen it happen again and again. A person gets in a tight spot and decides to turn to God. But when the pressure is off, he stops behaving wisely and begins to repeat his mistakes.

The Bible has a graphic way of describing what happens to those who refuse to walk in wisdom:

> **As a dog returns to his own vomit, so a fool repeats his folly.**
>
> **Proverbs 26:11**

> But it has happened to them according to the true proverb: "A dog returns to his own vomit," and, "a sow, having washed, to her wallowing in the mire."
>
> 2 Peter 2:22

Now, I understand that the visual picture those scriptures bring to mind is rather gross, but it gets the point across! If we don't keep operating in wisdom, we will eventually end up in the same kind of mess all over again.

We see Pharaoh making this mistake in Exodus 8. God raised up Moses as Israel's deliverer, sending him to tell Pharaoh to let His people go. When Moses came before Pharaoh with God's message, Pharaoh hardened his heart and refused to free the Israelites.

It became a war of wills between this one man, Pharaoh, and Almighty God. Pharaoh would harden his heart and refuse to let the people go, and God would send another plague. Pharaoh would relent in order to get relief from the plague. However, as soon as the plague ended and the pressure was off, he would harden his heart and once more refuse to obey God's command to release the children of Israel.

Exodus 8 relates the account of the second plague. Moses tells Pharaoh, "This is what God says: If you don't let His people go, He's going to send frogs, and it won't be two or three frogs. You will have more frogs than you ever wanted to see in your life! There will be frogs in your shoes, in your room, in your bed, in your kitchen, and in every drawer, bowl, and bag. There will be frogs everywhere!"

So the frogs came, and they *were* everywhere. The Egyptians couldn't go anywhere without seeing piles upon piles of frogs.

Finally, Pharaoh had had enough and called for Moses. When Moses came, Pharaoh said, "That's enough of the frogs! It's too much! I'll let your people go."

So Moses prayed, and God stopped the plague of frogs. All the frogs died except those left in the Nile River. The Egyptians scraped up all the dead frogs and piled them in great heaps.

Verse 14 goes on to say that the land stank — and that certainly isn't hard to believe! However, once the frogs were out of the way, Pharaoh felt relief and immediately hardened his heart again.

That's exactly what many of us do. When we find ourselves in a crisis, we call upon God. We tell Him that we'll never stray from Him again but will serve Him all the days of our lives.

But when the pressure starts to lessen, we are tempted to take advantage of God's mercy and stop behaving wisely. And if we're not careful, we will harden our hearts once more and eventually get ourselves in the same predicament we were in before!

Don't let yourself make that mistake, friend. You *can* keep walking in the wisdom you have gained from one season to the next. Just make the decision that you will do what the Word tells you to do, no matter what.

Only in the Word will you find the keys you need to get you out of that vicious cycle once and for all. Only by continually walking in wisdom can you move on over into your new future of promise and hope!

See Your Life
From God's Vantage Point

So how do we make sure we keep behaving wisely in every season of life? *We do whatever is necessary to make sure we are seeing life from God's vantage point.*

I once saw a bumper sticker that said, "Sometimes I wake up grumpy; other days I let him sleep in." I don't believe that bumper sticker should apply to a born-again, blood-bought child of God who is filled with the resurrection power of God! A believer shouldn't wake up day after day after day feeling depressed, grumpy, and sad and then excuse himself by saying, "Well, that's just the way I am." No, that person needs to change!

If that description sounds uncomfortably familiar, you need to ask yourself: *How long am I going to allow myself to stay discouraged and depressed? When am I going to stop carrying around these hurts and disappointments that should have long ago been left behind in a past season?*

All of us have those mornings when we wake up in a bad mood. Sometimes we wake up feeling a little out of sorts because we did something foolish like staying up until 2:15 in the morning eating pizza and drinking orange soda. But regardless of the reason we wake up on the wrong side of the bed, we need to shake off that bad mood so it doesn't become a pattern in our lives.

We always have the choice to see things from God's vantage point. So if we wake up in a bad mood, we should immediately do whatever is necessary to get the morning going in a different direction, whether it's taking a shower, brushing our teeth, or putting on some praise music. And if we keep on griping and complaining, we may need to do what my mama used to do to me when I "ran off at the mouth" — grab ourselves by the chin, walk ourselves to the sink, and wash our mouths out with soap!

WISDOM FROM ABOVE — THE PRINCIPAL THING

The Bible says that wisdom is the principal thing (Prov. 4:7) — the gift from God that we need most in this life. We don't need more money; we need wisdom. We don't need more time, more friends, or a "big break." *We need wisdom.*

If we gain wisdom, the other divine benefits we need will find their place in our lives. Wisdom will even bring those other benefits to us. Therefore, we should place our focus on this one goal: *to get wisdom.*

However, the wisdom we want is the wisdom from above. We *don't* want the natural wisdom that James 3:15 talks about, for that kind of wisdom is natural, earthly, sensual, and devilish. The vantage point of natural wisdom is below sea level. From that perspective, we can't see what's going on or where we're going.

I don't want to waste my time trying to discern, comprehend, and interpret my life from an earthly vantage point. I'd end up racing around the maze of life like a clueless rodent — back and forth in the same little rut, wearing out my tiny feet as I asked over and over, "Where is the cheese?" I want the vantage point from above, where Jesus is seated in the heavenlies! When I begin to see things from

His vantage point, I'll finally be able to say, *"There's* the cheese!"

But there is another wisdom that is from above. God's thoughts and ways are higher than our thoughts and ways. The vantage point He gives us provides an entirely different perspective of the problems and disappointments we face in life.

It all comes down to *God's way* versus *the way of the world*. We can adopt God's way of thinking, or we can limit ourselves to the world's way of thinking.

As long as we're still thinking the way the world is thinking, we're on dangerous territory, for the Bible says that even though the world was made through Jesus, the world didn't recognize Him (John 1:10). Also, in His prayer to the Father, Jesus said, *"O righteous Father! The world has not known You, but I have known You; and these have known that You sent Me"* (John 17:25).

If we're thinking like those who don't know God, we're never going to discover His wisdom and His ways. So how do we get our thinking aligned with God's way of thinking? By renewing our minds with His Word. As we stay in the Word, we will hear His thoughts, His plans, and His commandments, and we'll receive revelation from Him on how to live.

You have to understand that the Word of God is not just a book. It has the power to transform your life when you avail yourself to its truth on a regular basis. The more you expose yourself to the Word, the more it will change you and the more you'll start thinking the way God thinks. And *that* is what walking in wisdom is all about!

WORK VS. REST:
FINDING THE DIVINE ORDER

Wisdom sets a divine order in every arena of life. Regarding the arena of work, wisdom tells us this: *Don't try to rest when it's time to work.*

God established the pattern at creation. He worked; then He rested. Exodus 31:17 goes even further. It says that after God labored, He rested and *was refreshed*. The word "refreshed" means *to breathe and to be breathed upon.*[12]

> Regarding the arena of work, wisdom tells us this: *Don't try to rest when it's time to work.*

God is telling us the divine order: Once we work, we can then rest and be refreshed. But if we rest without working, we *won't* be refreshed.

Have you decided to "pick up the ax head" and get wisdom so you can move out of that tight, cramped space where you've been stuck for too long? If so, you will have to expend some effort. The blessings of God won't just come to you automatically. You will have to behave yourself wisely.

So when it's time to work, don't say, "I feel like I need to rest for a while so I can work hard later." No, you need to find out what God wants you to do and then do it; then after you've accomplished your task, you can rest and be refreshed.

---

[12] Ibid., #5312.

Don't make the mistake so many people make. They sit around waiting for something to happen without any effort on their part. Meanwhile, the Bible is telling *them* to go do something. For instance, Proverbs 6:6 says, *"Go to the ant, you sluggard! Consider her ways and be wise."*

Notice that this verse is talking to a "sluggard" or a lazy person. Proverbs 24:30 reveals to us that the sluggard is not only lazy, but also lacks understanding. As a result, his life is cursed. The word "curse" can mean to be *hemmed in with obstacles and powerless to resist*. Along this same line, my personal definition of the word "cursed" is *to be stuck in a season*.

Perhaps something negative happened to that person along the way. He developed a fleshly coping mechanism, and now it has turned into a stronghold that keeps him in bondage. It seems to him that he is stuck for life with that stronghold. He feels hemmed in with obstacles and powerless to resist — stuck in a season, cursed.

One of the primary ways a person can bring this state of being cursed on his life is to be lazy — to choose to rest when it's time to work. That's why God instructs the sluggard to "go to the ant."

Why is the ant the point of focus? Because the sluggard is so lazy that he's lying face down in a hammock, and the ant is the only thing in his line of vision that God can use to teach him something! So God tells the sluggard, "You lazy guy, look down at these ants. If you'll learn a lesson from them, you'll be a step closer to being wise!"

What was the lesson the sluggard needed to learn in order to gain wisdom? *When it's time to work, don't allow yourself to rest.*

However, there is another principle you have to understand if you're going to walk in God's divine order in this arena: *Don't work when it's time to rest.*

Just as there is a time to work, there is also a time to stop working — to take a sabbath, an intermission, a day of rest. If we don't take time to rest, there will come a day when we are forced to rest.

We can see this principle demonstrated in the Old Testament. God commanded Israel to rest the land, but the people refused to do it. Because of their repeated disobedience to the Lord in this and other areas, the Israelites went into captivity — and thus, the land rested.[13]

I have found in my own life that the times I get laid up in bed with symptoms of sickness always seem to follow times when I haven't rested the way I should. In other words, I experience a forced sabbath.

It's so important that we learn to be wise concerning this principle. On our jobs, we are to be hard workers. Whatever we put our hand to do, we are to do it with all our might. But when our task is complete, we must take the time to rest and get refreshed. In fact, our diligence in getting needed rest will make us better workers when it's time once again to "put our hand to the plow."

All of this is a part of behaving wisely in the affairs of life. As we follow God's divine order in this realm of work versus rest, we get ourselves in position for promotion and favor to come into our lives. There *is* a time to rest, but we must make sure we have fulfilled our assigned tasks first.

---

[13] *See* Leviticus 26:34,35.

THE SOURCE OF ALL WISDOM

Wisdom is available to us, but we have to go after it to get it for ourselves. But where does it come from? The Bible says wisdom comes *out of God's mouth*:

For the Lord gives wisdom; from His mouth come knowledge and understanding.

Proverbs 2:6

This also means that wisdom is found in the Word of God. However, you have to work at getting wisdom. It doesn't come by reading a scripture on your coffee mug or by going to church on Sunday morning. These are good things to do, but they're not enough.

You have to have a daily intake of the Word, for wisdom only comes out of God's mouth. Only He is wise. You're not going to get wisdom anywhere else. Dan Rather doesn't have it. You won't find wisdom on CNN or in *People* magazine. It comes only out of God's mouth and out of His Word, and you're the one who has to go get it.

> You have to have a daily intake of the Word, for wisdom only comes out of God's mouth.

Wisdom also doesn't come to you by osmosis. It won't come because you hang out in the Christian bookstore or carry your little pocket-sized Bible around with you. You have to deliberately expose yourself to the Word every day, planting its life-giving truth deep in your heart. There is no other way to get the wisdom you need in order to enter into God's good plan for your future.

Why is this true? Because where there's no Word, there's no faith. Where there's no faith, there's no anointing. Where there's no anointing, there are no burdens removed or yokes destroyed — and thus, you are left stuck in an undesirable season.

On the other hand, an intake of the Word brings faith; faith brings the anointing; and the power and anointing of God's Spirit causes burdens to be removed and yokes to be destroyed. At that point, my friend, you will move out of that undesirable season into a broad, open place where freedom reigns!

WISDOM FORESEES AND AVOIDS DANGER

In Proverbs 22:3, God gives us another reason why wisdom is so crucial in following His plan for our lives.

A prudent man foresees evil and hides himself, but the simple pass on and are punished.

Prudence is a very powerful, rich word in the Hebrew language. It means *to weigh; to form judgment; to have discretion; to use caution;* and *to behave wisely.*

The prudent person can foresee evil. In other words, he can discern or suspect when evil is ahead of him. And instead of continuing to head toward the danger, he turns away from that which would bring destruction to his life. If he takes a wrong turn, prudence helps him discern that the path doesn't look right so he can decide to adjust his course and get back on the right path.

That phrase "hides himself" in Proverbs 22:3 doesn't mean the prudent person is a coward. It means he is able to use discretion and discernment to navigate around danger. He thinks to himself:

- *Okay, I see that the drawbridge is up, so I'll wait before I forge on ahead.*
- *I see that there is a fallen tree in the road up ahead, so I'll take this detour.*
- *Danger is lurking there; I'm going a different way.*
- *Now is the time to move, so I need to get up and go quickly.*

A person who operates in prudence and wisdom can discern the bigger picture in a situation even if he doesn't know all the details. He is able to read the situation; he knows if there is something not quite right about it. As a result, he is able to determine the best course to take.

In contrast, people who lack prudence have no idea how to read a situation. That's why so many people will buy anything that they are told will make them rich, skinny, famous, or sexy. They'll see something advertised on television and immediately call to charge it on their credit card because they don't have any foresight. They're not looking ahead. And because they lack discernment and prudence, they read the situation incorrectly and end up wasting their money on something that does nothing but put them in greater debt.

DON'T GET 'CLOBBERED'!

I like the way *The Message* Bible puts Proverbs 22:3:

A prudent person sees trouble coming and ducks; a simpleton walks in blindly and is clobbered.

The wise person is able to foresee what lies ahead. Those who don't walk in wisdom often get "clobbered" because they *don't* look far enough ahead.

That was a principle I continually impressed on my oldest son as he was learning how to drive. I kept stressing to him that he shouldn't just look *around* him as he drove but *ahead* to the intersection or the brake lights in front of him. "To be a safe driver," I told him, "you have to have some foresight."

Every generation goes through a time when they don't look ahead but rather look only to the moment. Young people often give themselves over to the fun of the moment, without any foresight or desire to look ahead at what might happen as a consequence of their choices.

I am especially concerned in this respect with this present generation. The rise in popularity of extreme sports is just one example. No one seems to have told our young people that what goes up must come down!

I recently watched part of a television documentary on extreme sports and discovered that it is a very celebrated part of the sports world these days. On just about any day, you can look on ESPN2 and see people on bikes and skateboards flipping and flopping and doing all kinds of extreme tricks. Periodically you will see them crash.

The documentary I watched revealed the hidden part of extreme sports — the athletes who are now maimed and paralyzed from the neck down, in a "vegetable" state for the remainder of their lives. This isn't the celebrated, visible side of these sports that most people see. But it *is* a manifestation of what happens when people have no foresight. They just keep pushing the envelope out of boredom or for the applause of the moment, testing how close they can get to the edge without falling over. They don't think about the major consequences they could suffer because they are not exercising prudence.

You cause yourself many unnecessary problems when you allow a lack of foresight to pour over into your every-day life. For instance, you may decide, *Well, I'm mad, so I'm going to go spend some "mad money." I don't have any mad money saved, so I'll just charge my credit card to the ceiling!* Doing that may relieve your negative emotions for the moment. But if you thought you were depressed before you went out and spent that "mad money," just wait until your credit card bill comes!

People have all sorts of fleshly crisis mechanisms like that. For instance, some people think, *I'm feeling depressed, so I'm going to go raid the refrigerator!* They feel better for the moment, but then comes the letdown — the feelings of guilt and self-disgust. All these crisis mechanisms involve a lack of foresight. The only way a person can break out of these destructive patterns is to grow in God's wisdom so he can begin to have the prudence to see ahead.

CONSIDER WELL YOUR STEPS

Proverbs 14:16 has more to say about a person who has foresight and operates in wisdom.

> **A wise man fears and departs from evil, but a fool rages and is self-confident.**

Let's look at a few other translations of this verse:

A wise man is cautious and turns away from evil, but a fool throws off restraint and is careless.

Proverbs 14:16 *RSV*

A wise man is cautious and avoids danger; a fool plunges ahead with great confidence.

Proverbs 14:16 *TLB*

The wise watch their steps and avoid evil; fools are headstrong and reckless.

Proverbs 14:16 *Message*

Wisdom will help you to discern or suspect danger; it will help you consider well your steps and depart from the wrong way. You find that wisdom by getting into the Word and staying sensitive to the leading of the Holy Spirit, who is the very personification of wisdom. He will expose the wrong way and reveal to you the right way to go. He will help you walk circumspectly — not as a fool but as one who is wise (Eph. 5:15).

Don't Get Stuck
In *Trends* or *Traditions*

Walking through life as those who are wise includes not allowing ourselves to get stuck either in *trends* or *traditions*.

Many Christians make the mistake of getting stuck in a season because of man's traditions. Grandma taught it, and they bought it! But Jesus said in Matthew 15:6, "*...you have made the commandment of God of no effect by your tradition.*"

In other words, if what we believe doesn't line up with the Scriptures, it isn't going to help us, I don't care how sentimental we feel about it. Our lives have to line up with the Word of God.

Sometimes people would rather ignore the Word of God than let go of their traditions. For instance, once when I was engaged in a conversation with someone, the person said, "Well, I believe this way."

"But this is what the Word says," I responded.

The person replied, "Well, I don't care what the Word says; this is what *I* believe!"

That was a Christian who said that! I'm telling you, holding on to tradition at the expense of the Word will cause a person to make some very poor choices!

The other danger is to get stuck in the rut of being trendy. I want to caution you about this, because there is now more information available to us than ever before. Today almost anyone can publish a book or get on Christian television. So just because something is called Christian doesn't mean we should swallow it hook, line, and sinker!

There are a lot of trends that come along in the Body of Christ, and not all of them are bad. From time to time, God will emphasize a truth to get His people out of a ditch and back in the middle of the road where they need to be. But in dealing with these different areas of emphasis, the Body of Christ has become very "trendy" as a whole.

For instance, I watched one pastor friend of mine take his church from one spiritual trend to the next for years. He started out with a balanced ministry; then he began to put great emphasis on intercession in prayer. He eliminated all the other church activities except prayer meetings, including Bible studies and fellowships. In this pastor's view, there was no time for anything else because his congregation needed to *pray*.

Then another trend came along, and my minister friend grabbed on to it. This time it was the joy movement. When this trend hit his church, the congregation didn't get together to pray anymore. They didn't have to pray because they had the joy of the Lord as their strength! Now they could just come together and giggle in the Holy Ghost!

Now, don't misunderstand me — the joy movement was a good thing. The truth is, the Body of Christ needed to be perked up a little bit! But that didn't mean Christians were supposed to throw out all the other truths God had taught them and do nothing but get filled with joy and Holy Ghost laughter!

After the joy movement came another revival of spiritual warfare. With this new trend, people were no longer filled with joy — they were mad at the devil! Again and again, Christians have gone from one extreme to the next extreme as they follow the latest spiritual trends. If you watch them too closely, you'll get motion sickness!

God wants us to embrace both the old *and* the new, as long as what we embrace lines up with the Word. When a new spiritual trend comes along, we need to pay attention and ask God what He is saying to the Church. But even if we discern that the current emphasis on a certain truth *is* from God, that *doesn't* mean we are

> God wants us to embrace both the old and the new, as long as what we embrace lines up with the Word.

to forsake the other truths we have known all along. As Ephesians 4:14 says, *"...We should no longer be children, tossed to and fro and carried about with every wind of doctrine...."*

The key to life is *balance*. We are not to get stuck in man's traditions, nor should we get stuck in a self-imposed race to find the next spiritual trend. If we want to stay in God's will from one season to the next, we can't simply buy into everything that comes out on Christian television or in Christian books. We must always be discerning, judging everything we hear by the Word of God.

Some traditions and some trends are wonderful, but if you're stuck in either one of these, you'll never get out of the season you're in right now. Neither traditions nor trends carry the key that will open the door for you.

WISDOM HOLDS THE KEYS

The bottom line is this: You must always listen on the inside for the Spirit of Truth. He will keep you both in balance and in wisdom. Wisdom holds the keys for getting out of the season you don't desire and for getting into the season you do desire. For real and lasting change in your life, you're going to have to do what the Bible says and *get wisdom*.

> **Wisdom is the principal thing; therefore get wisdom. And in all your getting, get understanding....**
> **I have taught you in the way of wisdom; I have led you in right paths.**
> **When you walk, your steps will not be hindered, and when you run, you will not stumble.**
> **Take firm hold of instruction, do not let go; keep her, for she is your life.**
>
> **Proverbs 4:7,11-13**

> Happy is the man who finds wisdom, and the man who gains understanding;
>
> For her proceeds are better than the profits of silver, and her gain than fine gold.
>
> She is more precious than rubies, and all the things you may desire cannot compare with her.
>
> Length of days is in her right hand, in her left hand riches and honor.
>
> Her ways are ways of pleasantness, and all her paths are peace.
>
> She is a tree of life to those who take hold of her, and happy are all who retain her.
>
> **Proverbs 3:13-18**

Let me remind you of the way you get wisdom: *Wisdom comes out of God's mouth.* You must have a daily intake of and daily exposure to the Word of God. You must also call out to God and invite the Holy Spirit to lead you. As you ask for wisdom, God will give it to you liberally (James 1:5). You don't have to know all the details, but the Holy Spirit will show you whatever you do need to know as you go from one season to the next.

Run After Wisdom

Suppose I told you I held the key that would open the door to get you out of the mess you're in and take you to a better place. But then I took off running with that key still in my hand! Would you chase me? Sure you would! You'd go after that key as fast as you could go!

Well, wisdom holds the key, not only to get you out of the prison cell you're confined to right now, but to open the door to a broad, open, beautiful place in the next season of your life. If you really believe that, you'll run after wisdom.

You'll climb over walls and run through swamps if need be. You'll do *anything* to go get wisdom!

That's the kind of desire you have to have in your heart if you want to change your situation. You can't live your life behaving unwisely and still expect to leave where you are to enter into a new and better season.

So make the decision to *go get wisdom.* There *is* a way out, and wisdom holds the key!

ON YOUR WAY
TO THE
NEXT SEASON

4

*A*s you get ready to leave an old season, it's important for you to understand that you can't enter into a new season empty-headed. There are some things you have to know in order to flow from one season to the next as God has ordained for you.

For one thing, *you need to know that you can make it.* You should never again say, "I just can't make it. I'm about to cave in under all that has been happening in my life." Don't say that any more. You *can* make it out of the season you're in. You *can* enter into the future season of hope that is waiting for you.

In First Corinthians 10:13, God gives you His rock-solid assurance on this matter:

> **No temptation has overtaken you except such as is common to man; but God is faithful, who will not allow you to be tempted beyond what you are able, but with the temptation will also make the way of escape, that you may be able to bear it.**

The word "temptation" in this verse means *temptation, test,* or *trial.* It has to do with circumstances and adversity in life that are not enjoyable — things that God never intended for us to experience.

Notice that God says *no* temptation has come upon you but such as is common to man. It's a trick of the devil to make you think that your situation is somehow unique and worse than anyone else's problems. That just isn't true. You need to know that any challenge you face has been faced by countless others through the ages. You are no special, hopeless case to God!

You also need to establish this fact deep in your heart: *God is not the author of your problems.* Sometimes your problems come from the enemy; sometimes they come from you. But God is *never* your problem. You have to believe that beyond a shadow of a doubt if you're ever going to find His way of escape from the old season you've been trapped in for so long.

> ...Establish this fact deep in your heart: *God is not the author of your problems.*

Here's another truth you have to know: *What you're going through is NOT more than you can bear.* It is a lie of the enemy that says you can't bear the pressure. *God* says that with the temptation, test, or trial, He is faithful not to allow more to come upon you than you are able to bear!

The *Amplified Bible* says that "...*no temptation or trial has come to you that is beyond human resistance and that is not adjusted and adapted and belonging to human experience, and such as man can bear....*" God didn't bring the problem to you; however, He does allow it to come your way. But as it comes your way, He will intervene with a buffer of divine grace. In other words, if the trial *is* more than you can bear, He will adapt it and adjust it so it cannot take you out.

I don't care what the situation is that you're facing, *it is not too much for you.* It is not too big for you. You can make it out of that old season victoriously!

That's another thing you need to know: *God has provided you with a way of escape. The Amplified Bible* puts it this way: *"...With the temptation He will [always] also provide the way out (the means of escape to a landing place)...."* Start looking for the way out that God has provided for you.

I recently heard in the news about a couple of pilots in a B-1 airplane who were at 15,000 feet when their plane malfunctioned and they had to eject. Now, that would be a ride! That plane wasn't going eleven miles an hour! It was careening along *fast* at a *very* high altitude when those pilots experienced the malfunction!

One of the pilots reported that his sudden ejection from the disabled airplane was the worst jolt of his life. But I'll tell you what — on his way down, that same pilot was thinking, *I'm so glad to be out of there!* Pilots are trained to take that way of escape in case of emergency — and because they did, they came to a safe landing place.

Sometimes our divine way of escape from a bad situation is a "suddenly," much like the one those pilots experienced as they ejected from their imminent crisis. Significantly, one meaning of the Hebrew word for "delivery" or "rescue" is *to snatch out* with the implication that it happens *suddenly*. [14]

---

[14] Strong, "Hebrew Dictionary of the Old Testament," #5337.

We all like those "suddenly" deliverances, don't we? We may have been praying and crying and worrying about a difficult situation in our lives for days, and then *suddenly*, we wake up one morning and the entire situation has changed for the better! When that happens, we need to thank God for it and mark it in our memories for future reference. That way when we face new problems in the future, we can spend less time fretting and worrying and more time praising God for the way out that He's already provided!

We have all experienced some "suddenlies" in our lives. However, God's more common "way of escape" comes in steps. As I mentioned before, the process of coming out of a season is usually progressive. We see this concept reflected in another Hebrew word for "deliver" that means *to slip out and escape*, which implies a divine way of escape from a test or trial that is taken *by steps* and that takes some time.[15]

But whether your way out of an old season is a "suddenly" or one that is taken by steps, the truth you have to *know* is that *you are going to come out of it*. Don't just sit around waiting for your "suddenly." Start looking for God's exit sign *out* of that situation; then determine to follow Him step by step as He leads you to the next season of blessing and hope!

DON'T GIVE UP BEFORE YOUR 'DUE SEASON'

Remember what Galatians 6:9 says: *"And let us not grow weary while doing good, for in due season we shall reap if we do not lose heart."* This is another truth we need to establish in

---

[15] Ibid., #6403.

our hearts: *If we don't lose heart — if we don't cave in and quit — we will reach our "due season."*

One way or another, you will come out of your difficult situation if you'll just keep doing the right thing. I don't care how big the problem is, God will help you find the way of escape and His path to your "due season."

> *If we don't lose heart — if we don't cave in and quit — we will reach our "due season."*

You may be deep in debt; you may be dealing with a string of bad doctor's reports. Some of your most important relationships may be all knotted up in a tangle of strife and misunderstanding. But whatever is messed up, broken, or missing in your life right now, *assign it to this season.* Understand that it cannot run you over; it cannot hold you under until you lose your breath; it *cannot* take you out. You may be knocked *down*, but you are not knocked *out*. You are going on to the next season in God!

HOW TO RESPOND TO THE STORMS OF LIFE

Something else we need to know in order to enter our next season is what to do when we find ourselves in the midst of a storm. The fact of the matter is, storms come to all of us in life. It goes with the territory of living on this earth. But the good thing about storms is that they don't last forever!

Some storms are worse than other storms. Some storms you can see coming; others just come on you all of a sudden. But regardless of the kind of storm that blows into your life, there are three things you need to do when it hits.

First, when you're in a storm, *speak forth the command of faith and rebuke it.*

Mark 4:35-41 relates the time when a huge storm arose while Jesus and His disciples were sailing across the Sea of Galilee. The disciples woke up Jesus, who was sleeping peacefully in the bottom of the boat, and asked Him, "Master, don't You care that we are perishing?"

I imagine that the look Jesus gave His disciples as He got up was *not* a look of approval. Nevertheless, He stood up on the boat and rebuked the wind. Then He spoke to the waves, saying, "Peace, be still." At Jesus' command of faith, the winds stopped and the waves became calm.

You may say, "Yes, but that was Jesus! I can't rebuke a storm like *He* can!" But if that were true, why would Jesus have said what He did to His disciples right after the storm died down? He turned to them and said in effect, *"What's wrong with your faith?"* He was letting the disciples know that, instead of getting in fear, they should have used the authority He had given them to make the storm obey their command of faith!

So when you're in a storm, give the command of faith based on the authority in the Name of Jesus. That authority isn't based on *your* name or performance; it is based on your faith in His Name. You need to stand in that authority without wavering and *speak forth* your faith!

Don't ever keep your mouth shut during a storm! You need to square up against those stormy circumstances and declare, "In the Name of Jesus, I rebuke this storm in my life! I command you to be still! Every assignment of evil that has been arrayed against me, I render you powerless in the Name of Jesus. You've done all the destruction you're going to do because I resist you steadfastly in Jesus' Name. Greater is He who is in me than he that is in the world!"

Now, you can't be a sissy about it when you speak. You have to do it with *faith* and with *boldness*. You need to reach down on the inside and draw up the faith that is planted deep in your heart — faith that is fueled by the Word of God and the Spirit of God. Then in the authority given to you in the Name of Jesus, you have to stand up, square up, grit your teeth, get an attitude of "bulldog tenacity" on the inside, and *rebuke* that storm! Don't just let the storm throw you around and from side to side until all your resistance has eroded away. Tell it to *stop*!

Second, when a storm hits your life, *you must be quick to repent.*

In Jonah 2, we find that the prophet Jonah had gone his own way. As a result, he found himself in the belly of a great fish that God had prepared for him! Don't you know there were all kinds of unpleasant things — stomach acids, other unfortunate sea creatures, decomposing seaweed — that Jonah had to deal with in that fish's belly?

But Jonah made the right decision as he lay in that self-imposed mess: *He turned back to God and repented for his disobedience.* And it wasn't long before that fish became nauseated and vomited Jonah up on the shore! In the same way, you will nauseate *your* enemy when you turn around and get things right with God.

Sometimes a person finds himself in a storm because he is a goldfish and he's trying to act like a salmon. He doesn't understand why everything is coming against him, but the truth is, he's heading upstream in the wrong direction!

Well, that's why repentance is so important when you find yourself in the midst of a storm. The word "repent" means *to turn around*. That means you need to turn around and change the way you are thinking, talking, and acting. Change any wrong attitude, and get lined up with the direction and the flow of God. As you do, you will find that your repentance has a *great* and often *quick* impact on the storm that has come against you!

Third, *you need to ride out the storm.*

Sometimes you just have to hold on and forget about your wig and your new shoes. They may get ruined in the rain, but you can get a new wig in the next season! Rebuke that storm, and repent of anything in your life that may have helped bring the storm into your life. But realize also that there will be times when you just have *to hold on* to your faith and *ride out the storm* till it finally blows over.

In Acts 27, we read about a storm that arose at sea while Paul was a prisoner on a ship traveling to Rome. The Bible says the storm was so strong that, in an effort to keep the ship from sinking, the people threw all excess cargo and equipment over the side and undergirded the ship with cables to hold it together. Then the angel of the Lord came and stood by Paul. The angel told Paul that although the ship would run aground, no one would lose his life.

Do you know what that tells me about the storms we go through in life? *If we will just hold on, we will make it.*

The angel's message to Paul came to pass. As soon as the ship crashed on the shore, Paul and some of the others were walking around gathering up bundles of wood so they could warm themselves by a fire. In other words, the ship may have run aground, but it wasn't like all the people on board were injured and laid out on the rocks. They made it to the shore without harm!

Sometimes you just have to hold on, friend. If you don't quit and bail out, you will make it.

So always rebuke the storm; always repent; and realize that sometimes you just have to ride it out, knowing that your situation *will* get better. You will enter another season. Remember, you are called to go from where you are now to a better place. You are called to go from faith to faith, from strength to strength, from victory to victory, and from glory to glory.

This is what you have to know if you're going to move on to the next season. You have to get it in your thinking that you are *not* going down. For you as a believer, life isn't about going down, down, down in defeat. It's about seeing the hand of God move on your behalf, despite what is going on around you. It's about experiencing His favor, even if ten thousand fall at your right hand. It's a matter of allowing God to make a big difference in your life, just the way He loves to do it!

> You have to get it in your thinking that you are *not* going down.

So develop some strong faith and resolve on the inside by telling yourself, "I am *not* in this Christian walk to decrease. I'm not in it to get worn out and just barely float up to shore. I'm going to make it — and I'm going to look like something when I get there because I'm going from faith to faith, from strength to strength, from victory to victory, and from glory to glory!"

DETERMINE YOUR DIRECTION

To move from this season to the next, you must next *determine your direction*. You must have a sense of where you're going in life. You can't just wander around aimlessly and expect to get somewhere. You might accidentally get somewhere, but you won't stay there very long!

Maybe the devil has been lying to you. Perhaps the people around you have given you advice based on their own experience, saying, "Accept it — there is no way out; that's just the way you are. That's your lot in life."

You need to resist those voices and come into a deeper knowledge of God's Word so He can show you the way out. Then you have to set the direction for your life, knowing that your situation *can* change. It can be totally fixed, altered, redeemed, created — whatever it takes to bring you out of the old season into a better, more desirable season of life.

Proverbs 14:12 says, *"There is a way that seems right to a man, but its end is the way of death."* Next to that verse, I've written in my Bible, "Good ideas versus *God* ideas."

> It is very important that we don't just wander into a good idea and end up committing our lives to something that takes us in the wrong direction.

Let me tell you — there is a vast difference between good ideas and "God ideas." It is very important that we don't just wander into a good idea and end up committing our lives to something that takes us in the wrong direction. That is easy to do in this age of information. Just about anyone can get on the Internet these days. In addition, there are books, magazines, CDs, and 1-800 numbers that can give you information on just about any subject you can imagine.

But if we buy into every good idea that is out there in the world, our time, energy, and resources will be scattered all over the place and, as a result, we will be neither effective nor productive in our pursuits. That's why we don't want to just gather information on what "they say" or from "www.know-it-all.com"; we want to find the "*God* idea" for our lives.

Ultimately, I don't want to ever be in the position of thinking I delivered myself with my own good ideas. *God* is my Deliverer and my Champion, so whenever I come out on top of any problem or difficult situation, I make sure to declare that it was God who did it for me.

Sometimes after we achieve a goal we've been striving for, we are tempted to think, *Man, we worked real hard, and we sustained ourselves through all the hardships. We did it!* No, it was God who helped and sustained us till we reached that goal. He is our Deliverer. He is our Champion. We must never let ourselves get confused on this point. When people ask us, "How were you able to accomplish this?" we shouldn't reply, "Well, I figured this out; I looked this up; I worked on this." We need to say, "God did it. I couldn't have done it without Him." That's the wise position to take; that's the safe place to be.

We talked about pursuing wisdom earlier. Simply put, wisdom is actually knowing *what* God wants and *how* He wants it. We can pursue wisdom, or we can pursue the way that seems right. But if we want to go on to a better season, we can't settle for a direction that "seems right"; we have to have the real deal. We have to make sure that the direction we're headed *is* right — that it is the God idea for our lives.

Take It Step by Step

As I mentioned earlier, once you get on the right path and start moving in the right direction, you'll begin to move toward a better future by steps. You won't just suddenly slide to the finish line the first day!

Of course, I believe there are times that as we endeavor to walk out God's plan step by step, He just picks us up by the belt and moves us ahead thirty spaces. But that is only at His discretion and for His purposes. For the most part, we walk down His path one step at a time by faith.

Look at what the Bible says about this step-by-step process into the good future God has planned for us:

> **The steps of a [good] man are directed and established by the Lord when He delights in his way [and He busies Himself with his every step].**
> **Though he falls, he shall not be utterly cast down, for the Lord grasps his hand in support and upholds him.**
>
> **Psalm 37:23,24 *AMP***

> **Trust in the Lord with all your heart, and lean not on your own understanding;**
> **In all your ways acknowledge Him, and He shall direct your paths.**
>
> **Proverbs 3:5,6**

The literal Hebrew says that God will make your path *smooth*. God will help you set your direction, and He will smooth out the path before you as you start moving forward. Nevertheless, you will still reach your destination *by steps.*

Years ago when my wife and I were still living in Tampa, the Lord was really ministering to my heart about moving to Ocala to start a church. One day I was getting on a highway in north Tampa when I saw a big green sign that said, "Next Right Ocala."

Now, I didn't see that as a sign from Heaven. The truth is, the matter was all but settled; my family and I were getting ready to make the move. I had already surrendered to what God wanted me to do. I just thought the sign's message was kind of humorous, given my circumstances. It also confirmed to me what I already knew in my heart: The "next right" thing for me to do in life was to go to Ocala, Florida, and start a church. And, of course, the rest is history!

So how does that illustration apply to your life? Well, God is saying to you that you can leave the season you're in. You're free to depart from evil and to behave wisely. As you do, your "next right" will be peace! Pursue that divine peace with all your heart, for where you find peace, you'll find the desirable season God has for you.

Establish Your Vision

Once you receive *direction* from God, that direction establishes your *vision*. This is a crucial key to entering a new season, for Proverbs 29:18 (*KJV*) says, "*Where there is no vision, the people perish....*"

When I say "vision," I'm not talking about a desired dream or a goal you've set for yourself. Vision isn't just a goal you want to reach; it isn't just thinking about what you want to do or what you want to have in the next season up ahead of you. *Vision is what you can see.*

Now, in order to see, we have to have light. Where do we find that light? Psalm 119:105 tells us: *"Your word is a lamp to my feet and a light to my path."* Verse 130 goes on to say, *"The entrance of Your Word gives light...."*

You won't be able to see without the Word of God, for it's the Word that gives you a vision for your life. This is one of the main reasons it's so important to maintain a daily exposure to and intake of the Word of God — because you have to see yourself in the next season of life before you'll ever get there.

You have to see what God sees for you, and you'll only find that vision in the Word of God. It's like putting on spiritual "virtual reality goggles." When you're looking through your Word goggles, you can see yourself well, free, happy, blessed, strong, confident, and fruitful in everything you set your hand to do. You can see yourself surrounded with favor and successful in possessing your promised land. But you can only see yourself this way when you allow the Word to shed the light of its truth upon your life.

So let me ask you this, friend: *Can you see yourself in the next season?* Don't answer that question flippantly; let your mind process what I'm asking you.

You see, if you can't see yourself on the other side of your situation, you'll have a hard time getting there. If you've been broke and sad, you have to see yourself provided for and happy. If you've been sick, you have to see yourself healthy and whole. If you're in business, you have to see your business succeeding. You can't just want your life to be better. You have to focus on where you want to go.

> *...If you can't see yourself on the other side of your situation, you'll have a hard time getting there.*

If you're grumpy, frumpy, and bumpy, can you see yourself free and happy? If you're in debt up to your belly button, can you see yourself debt-free? If you're fighting symptoms of sickness and disease and you've had some bad doctors' reports, do you see yourself free, healthy, strong, vibrant, and full of energy — or do you see yourself steadily deteriorating?

What do you see? I'm not talking about wishful thinking that says, *Oh, I want to be free. Oh, man, I want to be!* I'm asking you: *Can you actually see yourself free from this old season?*

What image do you have on the inside of where you're at right now? Do you see yourself succeeding and finding favor at your job, or do you see yourself as a "nothing ever goes right for me" type of person?

What do you see for your family? No matter what shape your marriage is in right now, do you see your relationship with your spouse becoming more intimate and loving? No matter what your children are doing right now, do you see them serving God? Do you see God's plan and design for their lives coming to pass?

Can you see yourself free from those habits or wrong attitudes that have bound you? Can you see yourself leaving a cloud of dust as you peel out from those places where you've made a mess and left a trail of trash behind you?

Can you see yourself moving on to a broad, free, wide-open place in a better season? Have you decided, "I've been here long enough — this place is just too tight and cramped for me"?

Can you see yourself confident? Can you see yourself bold and happy and feeling good about things? Or do you still see yourself as the little kid who never could get things right, the one whom people picked on in the playground?

What do you see? That is an extremely important question to answer, for *what you see will determine your course and your direction in life*. You have to get a vision on the inside. You have to be able to *see*.

STAY FOCUSED!

Once you see where you're supposed to be headed in life, you have to *focus* on that vision and *stay* focused.

One of my assistant pastors once bought me a telescope for Christmas. On this telescope is a viewfinder that helps a person find what he's looking for. On the night we pulled out the telescope to use it, Jupiter was close enough to earth for us to see it through the telescope. So we used the viewfinder to lock in on Jupiter; then we focused the lens so we could see the planet as clearly as possible.

That's the way it works in the arena of vision. First, you have to *see* your destination up ahead of you. Then once you see it, you have to *focus* in on it. This is vital to understand, for you will always move toward your point of focus, and you will accomplish whatever you stay focused on.

James 1:8 says that a person without focus is *"...a double-minded man, unstable in all his ways."* The *Amplified* version puts it this way:

> **For truly, let not such a person imagine that he will receive anything [he asks for] from the Lord,**
>
> **[For being as he is] a man of two minds (hesitating, dubious, irresolute), [he is] unstable and unreliable and uncertain about everything [he thinks, feels, decides].**

> ...You will always move toward your point of focus, and you will accomplish whatever you stay focused on.

James 1:7,8 *AMP*

The word "double-minded" in the Greek actually carries the meaning of *isolating; going back and forth; being of two spirits; being of two minds;* and *trying to look in two directions at the same time.* That is definitely *not* a good condition to be in as you go through life. If you're always trying to look in two directions at the same time, you're eventually going to get very dizzy and confused! If you want to move forward to the next season, you will have to set your direction, establish your vision, and then *focus* on your destination. That is the *only* way you will ever get to the next season in God.

SET YOUR FACE LIKE A FLINT

So what are we to set our focus on? Of course, first we must set our focus on Jesus. Hebrews 12:1,2 tells us to look away from the things that distract us from our walk with God and to look to Jesus instead. But we are also to look to

115

Jesus because He is the supreme Example and the Master at staying focused. That's what the Bible is talking about when it says Jesus "set His face like a flint":

> "I gave My back to those who struck Me, and My cheeks to those who plucked out the beard; I did not hide My face from shame and spitting.
> "For the Lord God will help Me; therefore I will not be disgraced; THEREFORE I HAVE SET MY FACE LIKE A FLINT, and I know that I will not be ashamed."
>
> **Isaiah 50:6,7**

Jesus went through so much in those last few days of His life. He suffered beatings; He endured the mocking of people who spat on Him and pulled out His beard. The Bible said He underwent such anguish and such pressure that He sweat "...*as it were great drops of blood falling down to the ground*" (Luke 22:44 *KJV*).

In medical history, there are rare cases recorded of people who have actually sweat blood. This condition is brought on by incredibly severe mental anguish and pressure that causes a person's pores to dilate and release both sweat *and* blood.

Jesus was under this kind of intense pressure in the Garden of Gethsemane. He knew He was about to take on the sins of mankind. To go through this ordeal, He would have to go through a horrific gauntlet of focus-breakers, including the worst kinds of torture. All of this was lined up for Him to experience in the hours that lay ahead as He knelt there praying in the Garden. *But Jesus refused to lose His focus.* Hebrews 12:2 says, "...*For the joy that was set before Him* [He] *endured the cross....*"

Jesus' focus was on the throne, not the Cross. He endured everything else, setting His face like a flint, because of the joy that was set before Him. Flint is a hard and unyielding substance, which gives us a picture of Jesus' determination to stay focused. He made the firm decision, "I'm not going to move off this course the Father has set for me. I am headed toward what I see!"

We can't imagine the kind of pressure Jesus went through that night, but we can all relate to pressure. We've all had times of pressure when we were hit by adverse circumstances from every side, when it felt like someone put the weight of the whole world on our backs.

During times of intense pressure, you might not know how you're going to make it. But if you will follow Jesus' example by focusing on the joy set before you, God will lift you up and help you begin to see your future and your hope. You'll begin to think, *I'm coming out of this!* And as you set your face like a flint toward the goal, you will come out of that stormy season victoriously.

Just as Jesus had to deal with all kinds of focus-breakers, so will you. There are literally a million focus-busters in this world, all vying for your attention, not the least of which is the fear of failure. You will also have to deal with voices from your past as well as voices from the present — from your peers, your family, your coworkers, and your friends.

Sometimes more significant than what people say is that little look they give you when you say, "Well, I'm believing God for this," and they reply with a complete lack of enthusiasm, "Oh, well. Praise God." That is why you shouldn't share the vision God has given you with just anyone. Such important matters should be shared only with people of like precious faith.

All kinds of things will threaten to break your focus. But no matter what, you must determine to keep your eyes fixed on the goal, because *whatever you stay focused on, you will accomplish.*

That means your problem is not your *problem* — your problem is *your lack of focus.* To help you understand what I mean by that, see if this scenario sounds familiar: First, you come to understand the direction you should go. You begin to see on the inside what you are supposed to be doing. You even set your focus on that vision — but then you mess up, get off track, and lose your focus.

If that describes your situation, don't just resign yourself to failure —determine to get your focus back! Go back through the entire process again. Hear from God again; see what God has for your future again; and then set your focus on that vision. But this time, *refuse* to let *anything* distract you!

Make the quality decision, "I will not retreat, and I will not argue about this anymore! I'm headed toward what I see — the abundance and wholeness that God has for me and mine!"

Sure, there will be distractions and temptations that come along to throw you off course as you move toward that goal. That's why you have to *set your face like a flint.*

Just as God helped Jesus stay focused despite all He went through, God will help you stay focused as you take in the life-changing, transforming power of His Word. Your part is to begin to gather wisdom from God. Get divine direction for your situation. Make the decision that you won't mindlessly wander through life saying, "I sure have a lot of problems." Instead, you'll do something to get back on course!

Sit down and conduct an inventory of what needs to change in your life. Then push back all distractions, and find some time in your life to discover what God is saying about your mess. Don't just read the Word — let the Word speak to *you*.

Proverbs 4:20-27 (*NIV*) tells you what will happen if you'll set your focus on what God has to say:

> **My son, pay attention to what I say; listen closely to my words.**
> **Do not let them out of your sight, keep them within your heart;**
> **for they are life to those who find them and health to a man's whole body.**
> **Above all else, guard your heart, for it is the well-spring of life.**
> **Put away perversity from your mouth; keep corrupt talk far from your lips.**
> **Let your eyes look straight ahead, fix your gaze directly before you.**
> **Make level paths for your feet and take only ways that are firm.**
> **Do not swerve to the right or the left; keep your foot from evil.**

In other words, as you keep God's Word continually before your eyes, His wisdom will bring health and wholeness to your life, and He will lead you on a smooth path all the way to the next season!

That's what vision is all about. You find out what God is saying about your situation; then you begin to develop on the inside the image of what He has for you. Once you see yourself in the wonderful future God has prepared for you, you have to *seize it* by faith; *set your focus* on it; and then *head toward it* with all your strength!

TRUST IN GOD'S TIMING

Let's look now at how we can *keep* our focus once we know what we are to focus on.

That is the crux of the problem — keeping our eyes fixed on our God-ordained destination in the midst of the many circumstances and distractions that come into our lives to interrupt and break our focus. But it is a challenge that has to be overcome, for what we stay focused on determines what we will accomplish and where we will end up in life.

I want to give you two key principles that will help you keep your focus, regardless of the circumstances that surround you. First, *trust the timing of God.* He wants to bring you out of that old season, but in His Kingdom, timing is everything. He knows that if everything came to you in an instant, you'd never have the opportunity to develop any character.

The truth is, time is one of the biggest focus-breakers of all. When time begins to come against us, it ticks very loudly, just as clocks seem to do at night when everything else is quiet. When that happens, too often we forget that in God, there is always a "due season" according to Psalm 104:27:

> **These all wait for You, that You may give them their food in due season.**

Do you see what we are to do when the due season has not yet arrived? *We are to wait.*

> **The eyes of all look expectantly to You, and You give them their food in due season.**
>
> **Psalm 145:15**

What are we to do? *Look expectantly to God.*

However, instead of waiting in faith, we often let time become our focus-breaker. We think, *I should have been delivered from this problem by now! I called out to God. I know what His will is. But I'm still here. Why is it taking so long?*

If we're not careful, we'll start to cave in at this point. We'll lose sight of our due season and start thinking about giving up. *But if we don't quit, we can't lose.* As Galatians 6:9 exhorts us, *"...Let us not grow weary while doing good, for in due season we shall reap if we do not lose heart."*

Recently I was talking to a precious brother in the Lord who had just gone through a year of incredible pain and loss. As I walked with him through part of that difficult season, I watched him come into a new intimacy with God he had never even imagined before.

During that year when I'd ask this man how he was doing, he'd replied, "I'm hanging on." Let me tell you, it's great to hang on in the midst of a storm! It's certainly a lot better than letting go! More than once, I reminded this brother in the Lord that he needed to allow for God and time — *not* just for time alone. Time alone is a torturer, but God and time together will help a person heal and become whole again.

In the beginning, this man seemed to be underwater, constantly fighting just to get some air. But he allowed for

121

God and time, and he just kept holding on. It wasn't long before he was able to touch the bottom again. And the time came when he walked out of the stormy waters into a broad, free place of healing and blessing.

You can do the same thing this man did. Don't let go when you're fighting to get through the storm. Just keep holding on as you allow for God and time. And before you know it, you'll be lying on the beach in a hammock, drinking lemonade and thanking God for a new season of freedom and peace!

You see, the devil just can't cope with our consistency. We just have to hang in there and continue to trust the timing of God, for the due season always comes. God can see more than we can see. He knows more than we know.

We may want to burst out of the gate running, but God may see a fast truck coming. Therefore, it is best to put on the brakes and *wait* on the Lord till we have that "green light" on the inside telling us it's time to take the next step.

So often we get ourselves in trouble by circumventing the timing of God — by not waiting for His provision or for His open door of opportunity. When we do that, we are in danger of creating a worse mess than when we started. That's why we need to make sure we are trusting God with the timing of our deliverance. He knows what we don't know; He sees what we don't see. And as we wait on Him, looking expectantly to Him for our answer, He will bring us out of our old season at the perfect time.

> ...We need to make sure we are trusting God with the timing of our deliverance.

That's exactly what David was talking about in Psalm 31:14,15:

> But as for me, I trust in You, O Lord; I say, "You are my God."
> My times are in Your hand; deliver me from the hand of my enemies, and from those who persecute me.

Notice what David said in verse 15: *"My times are in Your hand...."* He was saying that he was entrusting the days and seasons of his life into God's hands.

That is exactly what you must do as well as you set your sights on the next season. You have to throw off that natural tendency to make a mad dash to the next step without considering the consequences. Instead, just keep telling yourself, *God is never late or early. He is always on time. Therefore, I trust Him with the timing of my deliverance. His ways and His thoughts are higher than my ways and my thoughts. He has a much higher vantage point than I do. He can see what I cannot see.*

Yes, time may seem to be working against you, yelling in your ear, "This situation is supposed to be better by now!" But just keep trusting God with the timing of your deliverance. You don't want to get to the next season too soon; otherwise, when you arrive, there will be no fruit ripe for the harvest — and fruit that is picked before its time is bitter.

On the other hand, you don't want to get there too late; if you do, someone else will be eating your fruit. And if you get there *very* late, all the fruit will be gone! That's why you have to move with God. Put your times in His hand, and trust in His timing. Trust that as you call upon Him and let Him lead you, He will work on your behalf to bring you into your new season.

123

Keep Hope Alive

Second, you must keep hope alive. Remember, we're talking about keeping our focus. If hope wanes, you'll start focusing on other things and begin to lose your focus on what really matters. Soon you'll have no focus at all, and life will once again become a blur.

That was the condition David found himself in when he wrote Psalm 42:11:

Why are you cast down, O my soul? And why are you disquieted within me? Hope in God; for I shall yet praise Him, the help of my countenance and my God.

David is talking to himself in this scripture. Have you ever done that? It's actually good for you to talk to yourself — as long as you don't argue back!

David is asking himself a question that we all often ask ourselves as we go through life: "Why are you cast down, O my soul?" That phrase "cast down" has to do with *being depressed.* We may be Word people. We may be faith people who believe in the integrity of God's Word. We may call ourselves believers and overcomers in Christ. Nevertheless, we all sometimes deal with depression to one degree or another.

Suppose you see written instructions near an elevator button that say, *"Depress the Button."* What does that mean? It means you are to *press down* the button with your finger. Well, circumstances of life can sometimes press you down and make you feel a little depressed. Maybe someone was rude to you; the washing machine broke down; or you forgot to fulfill a commitment you had made. These kinds of irritations can start piling up until you're asking yourself, *What's bugging me? Why do I feel so low?*

But when you're feeling pressed down by life, make sure that you're "spring-loaded"! Don't let yourself *stay* down.

Learn a lesson from David. First, he identified the symptoms of depression in his life by asking himself why his soul was feeling downcast, disquieted, and agitated within him. Then he spoke to his soul, telling it what to do in order to get *out* of depression: *"...Hope in God...."*

You can do the same thing David did when you're feeling down. First of all, never say you're having a "down day." Why would you assign your negative feelings to a full day? If you're feeling down, throw off that depression and *get over it*. You can do it by keeping hope alive!

We all experience adverse circumstances at one time or another, but we don't have to let those circumstances push us down. We can push back! We should never tolerate feelings of discouragement and depression; if we do, those feelings will just get heavier and heavier.

No matter what has been making you feel bothered, irritated, or depressed, you can launch yourself right out of those negative feelings by acting on the same solution David found: *Tell yourself to hope in God.* Or as the *Living Bible* puts it: *Expect God to act.*

How are you going to keep your focus in the midst of circumstances that threaten to agitate and discourage you? *You're going to keep your hope alive by expecting God to act!*

Recall to Your Mind
God's Faithfulness in the Past

Lamentations 3:21-24 gives us another vital key for keeping our hope alive so we can keep our focus on the "joy set before us":

> **This I recall to my mind, therefore I have hope.**
> **Through the Lord's mercies we are not consumed, because His compassions fail not.**
> **They are new every morning; great is Your faithfulness.**
> **"The Lord is my portion," says my soul, "therefore I hope in Him!"**

Notice what verse 21 says: *"This I recall to my mind, therefore I have hope."* The word "recall" means *the act of summoning back; to bring to mind; to remember.* You may know what God has done for you in the past; you may have heard His Word preached countless times. But something happens when you consciously *recall* or bring back to mind those truths you already know. That act of recalling triggers faith in your heart and causes hope to come alive again!

Think about it, friend. Has God ever come through for you in the past? Has He ever shown Himself strong on your behalf when you faced what seemed to be an impossible situation? If you want to keep your focus in the midst of turmoil, you'll have to recall those precious memories and let them ignite new hope in your heart!

That's what God commanded His people to do. Over and over again, God commanded the children of Israel to teach their children and their grandchildren what He had done for them in the past. For instance, look at what Moses told the Israelites in Deuteronomy 6:21-24:

> **"Then you shall say to your son: 'We were slaves of Pharaoh in Egypt, and the Lord brought us out of Egypt with a mighty hand;**
>
> **'and the Lord showed signs and wonders before our eyes, great and severe, against Egypt, Pharaoh, and all his household.**
>
> **'Then He brought us out from there, that He might bring us in, to give us the land of which He swore to our fathers.**
>
> **'And the Lord commanded us to observe all these statutes, to fear the Lord our God, for our good always, that He might preserve us alive, as it is this day.'"**

This was a divine ordinance given to the children of Israel. They were to teach their children and their grandchildren all that God had done for Israel in generations past.

There the Israelites were — living in the land of promise after being brought out of Egypt by God's mighty hand of deliverance. But God told them, "Don't just let your children grow up enjoying the blessings of this land in ignorance. They need to know what I did to get you here!"

Jewish parents were to tell their children and grandchildren: "Living in this land of abundance didn't just happen. God delivered us from Pharaoh. He split the sea so we could walk through on dry ground; then He caused the waters to come down on the enemy that surely would have stomped on us without His help!

"God used a pillar of fire by night and a pillar of cloud by day to lead us through the wilderness. He rained down manna for us to eat when there was no fresh food. He caused quail to fly in hordes to the Israelite camp so we could eat meat. When we needed water to drink, God caused water to come up out of a rock. Truly God has done great things for us to bring us into this Promised Land!"

There was an important purpose behind this particular ordinance. You see, God wanted every Jew to see himself as a part of the Israelites' deliverance from Egypt, even if he was generations removed from that historical exodus. All Jews were to understand that the God who split the Red Sea for their forefathers was the same God whose power was active and alive in their lives as well. The God who performed mighty works on behalf of Abraham and Isaac was the same God they were serving.

That principle still holds true today. God is not decrepit, forgetful, or grumpy. He hasn't lost one ounce of His energy or vitality. Just as He healed people centuries ago, He will heal you today. The same God who split the Red Sea will split *your* "Red Sea" and help you walk through to the other side on solid ground!

That's why it's so important that we keep reminding ourselves, our children, and our grandchildren of all God has done in the past. We, too, must see ourselves as part of the Israelites' deliverance from Egypt, for that same mighty God is *our* God, and He is able to deliver us today!

Psalm 78:1-7 tells us the lasting benefits that will result from recalling to mind God's past mighty works to the next generation:

> **Give ear, O my people, to my law; incline your ears to the words of my mouth.**
> **I will open my mouth in a parable; I will utter dark sayings of old,**

> Which we have heard and known, and our fathers
> have told us.
>
> We will not hide them from their children, telling to
> the generation to come the praises of the Lord, and His
> strength and His wonderful works that He has done.
>
> For He established a testimony in Jacob, and
> appointed a law in Israel, which He commanded our
> fathers, that they should make them known to their
> children;
>
> That the generation to come might know them, the
> children who would be born, that they may arise and
> declare them to their children,
>
> That they may set their hope in God, and not forget
> the works of God, but keep His commandments.

As parents today, we need to do a better job of reminding our children of God's past mighty works. It is wonderful that they live in the midst of blessings, favor, and abundance, but we need to remind them that God is the Source of the blessings they enjoy. In fact, they should be glad they didn't come along any sooner than they did!

Even though we may be going through a difficult season at the moment, most of us can remember a time when we didn't have it as good as we do now. For instance, I remember the stinky, little mobile home Alicia and I lived in when we first started the church in Ocala. The mobile home belonged to my grandmother, who lived in it when I was a little kid. Back then Grandma's mobile home had seemed big, new, and beautiful. It also used to smell nice! But by the time Alicia and I moved into the home, it wasn't so nice to live in any longer — not that we weren't grateful to have *anything* to live in at the time!

One night I told my wife that I was going to cook supper; however, when I started looking around in the kitchen, I realized there was hardly anything for me to cook! I found two frozen chicken breasts in the freezer; then I looked in our little pantry and found a can of cream of mushroom soup and a can of tomato sauce. So I just mixed what I had all together, put it in the oven, and called it supper!

Later Alicia came in the kitchen, took one look at my thrown-together chicken concoction, and immediately declared that she was *not* going to eat chicken in pink sauce. In the end, we went to Hardee's for a hamburger because we really didn't have anything else in the house to eat. Thank God, the Gilligan family has come a long way since then!

So tell your children what God has done in the past and what He can do for them today. Read other people's testimonies to your children so they can know of the great ways God moves in His people's lives. And don't neglect to tell your children of the great things God has done in *your* life. They should know where you came from, what you've been through, and how God has helped you, for that will cause *them* to have hope in God.

Think back on your life. What past challenges have you overcome? Were you once sick with a serious disease? Did the doctors tell you that you would never get any better — yet today, you *are* better? If so, recall to your mind how you made it through that difficult season by the power and the grace of God.

Or perhaps you once went through a difficult financial struggle, and the creditors said they were coming to take everything you had because you couldn't pay your bills. You wondered how you were ever going to get out of that mess — but somehow, someway, God came through for you. As you recall how God moved on your behalf to get you out of that situation, your hope will come alive for Him to deliver you from your present situation as well!

The truth is, if the devil had had *his* way in our lives, every one of us would be dead by now. We've all done some pretty foolish things that should have caused us to crash and burn in life. *But God came through and delivered us time and time again.* He took care of us and protected us, even when we were out in the world living for ourselves.

These are the kinds of things you need to recall to mind. Have you been through some dark times? Have you suffered pain and heartache? Well, guess what — you made it! God brought you through. He was faithful! You have to recall that truth to mind on a regular basis, for as you do, it will cause hope to arise in your heart for your present season.

You may say, "Yes, but I'm going through a dark time right now." Don't focus on what you're going through right now. Begin to focus on what Jesus did for you through His death and resurrection. Remember that He brought you through in times past, and He will bring you victoriously through this present challenge as well.

David practiced this principle, even when he was just a teenager. When David first arrived at the battlefield, he observed the army of Israel hiding behind trees and rocks as a huge giant of a man stood taunting them, defying them and cursing their God. David took one look at the giant and said, "Let me fight him."

King Saul asked, "Why should I let you do that?" Understandably, King Saul had some doubts about the young man's ability to fight such a formidable foe.

David replied, "I used to tend sheep for my father. One day while I was out tending those sheep, a lion came and carried away one of the sheep in its mouth. But I rescued that sheep and then killed the lion! Another day a bear came and tried to take one of the sheep, but I killed that bear too. The same Lord who delivered me from the paw of the lion and from the paw of the bear will deliver me from the hand of this uncircumcised Philistine!" (1 Sam. 17:34-37).

Now, try to put yourself in David's shoes for a moment. There he was, out there in the fields all alone, playing on his harp and watching his sheep. All of a sudden Mufasa the lion comes walking toward the flock! But what did young David do? In the name of the Lord, he got up and tore that lion apart!

Then on another day, here comes a bear, heading for David's sheep with a hungry look in its eyes. Now, normally a teenage boy knows better than to mess with a bear. But David was determined to protect his sheep — and in the name of the Lord, he killed that bear too!

As David recalls these two events in his mind, he thinks, *That lion didn't have a covenant with God, but I do. That bear didn't have a covenant with God, but I do. This giant also has no covenant with God — but I do! Therefore, the same God who delivered me out of the paw of the lion and out of the paw of the bear will deliver me from the hand of this uncircumcised giant!*

What was David doing? He was recalling to mind what God had done for him in the past, stirring up his hope that God would do the same for him when he faced this much greater challenge.

The apostle Paul was operating in this same principle when he wrote Second Corinthians 1:8-10:

> **For we do not want you to be ignorant, brethren, of our trouble which came to us in Asia: that we were burdened beyond measure, above strength, so that we despaired even of life.**
>
> **Yes, we had the sentence of death in ourselves, that we should not trust in ourselves but in God who raises the dead,**
>
> **who delivered us from so great a death, and does deliver us; in whom we trust that He will still deliver us.**

Paul was saying, "We were pressured on every side until we just about wanted to die. We experienced such heaviness and such opposition that we felt pressed to the point of death. But even so, we kept our hope in God alive. We trusted in Him who delivered us, who still delivers us, and who will yet deliver us in the future!"

You can count on it — a million and four things will try to come against you to break your focus after you have set your direction and established your vision. But no matter what, stay determined to keep your focus. Trust God with the timing of that vision fulfilled; meanwhile, keep your hope alive and in the present tense by recalling to mind what He has already done for you. As you do, your confident expectation in God's ability and willingness to act on your behalf will break off every focus-breaker that comes along!

NEVER LEAVE A SEASON EMPTY-HANDED

Earlier I stated that you can't enter a new season empty-headed, and we've talked about many of the crucial truths you have to know before God can launch you into that future of hope He has prepared for you. However, I want to stress one more important truth that you *must* understand as you prepare to leave the old season you're in: *You are never to leave an old season empty-handed.* I mentioned this principle earlier, but because of its importance, I want to go into more detail.

You are never to come out of any season without a harvest. No matter what kind of season you've been going through, be determined to come out with *something* good to show for it. Come out with a better grip on your problems, a better rhythm to life, a greater knowledge of when to duck from the enemy's fiery darts. Come out with a greater gratitude for God's faithfulness or a greater desire to serve Him. Come out with a lesson learned, with new revelation, with a greater measure of wisdom. Come out of that old season with *something* positive that you can use in the next season!

The children of Israel spent 430 years in slavery and bondage to Egypt. As they came out of that long and difficult season, God promised them, "As I deliver you out of this, you will not come out of it empty-handed."

> **"And I will give this people favor in the sight of the Egyptians; and it shall be, when you go, that you shall not go empty-handed.**
> **"But every woman shall ask of her neighbor, namely, of her who dwells near her house, articles of silver, articles of gold, and clothing; and you shall put them on your sons and on your daughters. So you shall plunder the Egyptians."**
>
> **Exodus 3:21,22**

Exodus 12:36 tells us what happened when the time came for the Israelites' deliverance from Egypt:

> **And the Lord had given the people favor in the sight of the Egyptians, so that they granted them what they requested. Thus they plundered the Egyptians.**

God gave you that biblical example so you could get hold of this principle and determine for yourself that you will never come out of a season empty-handed. There is always something you can gain from what you've gone through. If the only thing you bring out of that old season is the broken shackle still attached to your leg, at least you'll have a nice chain from which to hang a pretty wind chime in the next season!

Turn Your Hurts Into a Harvest

Not only will you be taking a positive harvest with you from the season you're in right now, but there will also be some things God will ask you to leave behind. Some of those things you may even fight and scratch in an effort to keep. But just stay open to God, and He'll show you what is better left behind as seed to produce a much better harvest in the season to come.

This brings us to another important truth you need to know as you prepare to leave an old season: *You can turn your hurts into a harvest.* Only by going through *tests* can you end up with a *testimony*.

How does that work? Instead of staying immersed in pain, loss, resentment, and bitterness, you activate the law of seedtime and harvest — also

> You can turn
> your hurts
> into a harvest.
> Only by going
> through *tests*
> can you end up
> with a *testimony.*

135

called the law of sowing and reaping — by turning those negative experiences into seed.

You can take virtually anything and call it a seed. But you need to realize that *the seed you sow determines the harvest you reap.* As Galatians 6:7 says, *"Do not be deceived, God is not mocked; for whatever a man sows, that he will also reap."* Genesis 1:12 confirms this, telling us that seed produces after its own kind.

You can plant whatever you choose to plant in the garden of your life, but you *will* reap a return on that seed. Therefore, it is a very good idea if you make the law of seedtime and harvest work *for* you instead of *against* you! Turn those past hurts into seed by forgiving and releasing; then sow that seed for a harvest of blessing in a better future!

Sometimes the things you're trying to take into the next season you have already lost. These are the things that may be worth more to you if you sow them as seed rather than going to all the trouble of trying to get them back. I'm talking about anything of value to you that the enemy has used other people to take from you. You see, when a thief comes, he comes to take things that are of value. He doesn't pull a gun on you and say, "I want some Q-Tips! Give me all your pocket lint!" No, that isn't what a thief comes to steal. He wants something *valuable*, so he says, "Give me that watch. You have a gold tooth? I want that too."

The same thing is true of the chief thief, the devil. He only wants to steal what is of value to you. But the things he succeeds in stealing from you through other people is probably worth more to you if you turn them into seed than if you spent all your energy squabbling over them, trying to get them back.

You just need to *forgive* and *release*, knowing that God is the One who keeps the books. You may say, "This situation didn't go right for me. That should have been mine. This wasn't fair." But just remember this: God does a good job of keeping the books. You need to forgive and release, because if you don't, you'll become strapped to that season, and you'll continue to drag it around with you until you *forgive*, *release*, and *sow*.

Is it really possible to do this? Yes, Jesus set the example when He said in essence, "No one takes My life. I lay it down of My own choice" (John 10:18). Jesus sowed His life and as a result reaped many sons and daughters.

So if someone takes something from you, don't waste your time fussing and fuming about what you lost. Sow it as seed, and move on to a better season!

Let me give you an example from my own life. A number of years ago when traveling to Romania on a ministry trip, I took along an expensive digital video camera. That camera was stolen from me during that trip, which of course didn't make me very happy.

However, I had just recently studied this principle of forgiving and releasing, so I decided I was going to release that camera. I wasn't going to fume about it; I wasn't going to meditate on how to get back at Romania. I would just let go of that camera and sow it into the life of the person who took it. And just as God promised, we have reaped that camera many times over!

Today our church has state-of-the-art digital camera equipment that we use to record our services and send them out on our television program all across this country. We don't go on the air and ask people for anything. We decided from the beginning that our purpose is just to give out the Good News and let God provide for the needs of the ministry — and He has done just that!

I could still be fuming about that Romanian thief who stole my camera. But I love the Romanians. I'll go back and minister to them any chance I get. I decided I wouldn't allow that thief to steal from me; instead, I sowed the camera as seed into that person's life.

Whenever you forgive those who hurt you — whenever you release that offense by sowing it as seed — that seed *will* produce a good harvest in your life. You just have to make up your mind that *you will not stay hurt* and that *you will never lose*. You have to declare by faith, "I cannot be stolen from!"

You may remember the pain of the past, but the moment you choose to sow those hurts as seed, you begin to move *away* from their negative effect on your life and *into* a better future. That's how you turn your hurts, your misfortunes, and your disappointments into a mighty harvest of blessing in the seasons yet to come!

SOW FREELY —
REAP ABUNDANTLY

In Luke 6:27-30, Jesus had something important to say about this subject of sowing our hurts as seed for a future harvest. His words provide a balance that we would do well to understand:

> **"But I say to you who hear: Love your enemies, do good to those who hate you,**

"bless those who curse you, and pray for those who spitefully use you.

"To him who strikes you on the one cheek, offer the other also. And from him who takes away your cloak, do not withhold your tunic either.

"Give to everyone who asks of you. And from him who takes away your goods do not ask them back."

Now, Jesus' instructions in this passage of Scripture would seem to be very difficult to follow — unless, that is, you understand the full context of what He's teaching here. Jesus isn't telling us to just let people run all over us and take all our possessions. We can get a better idea of what He *is* saying by reading further:

"But love your enemies, do good, and lend, hoping for nothing in return; and your reward will be great, and you will be sons of the Most High. For He is kind to the unthankful and evil.

"Therefore be merciful, just as your Father also is merciful.

"Judge not, and you shall not be judged. Condemn not, and you shall not be condemned. Forgive, and you will be forgiven.

"Give, and it will be given to you: good measure, pressed down, shaken together, and running over will be put into your bosom. For with the same measure that you use, it will be measured back to you."

Luke 6:35-38

So often we take verse 38 out of context and say, "If I give, it will be given to me — good measure, pressed down, shaken together, and running over!" But the previous verses tell us the other conditions that must be fulfilled in order to make that claim. God tells us, *Be kind to the unthankful; be merciful; don't judge; don't condemn; forgive others; give freely."*

139

All these commands point to the law of sowing and reaping. That means as you freely sow seeds of mercy, forgiveness, and material blessings into other people's lives, you get yourself in position to receive the promise of verse 38 — an abundant harvest of blessings that is *good measure, pressed down, shaken together, and running over*!

Remember, Jesus said, "You can't take My life; I lay it down of My own accord" (John 10:18). Follow the Master's example as you deal with the hurts and disappointments of the undesirable season you're trying to leave behind. Instead of focusing on your past hurts and offenses, activate the law of seedtime and harvest for your future benefit! Choose to forgive and release those who have wronged you. Sow that which you have lost as seed, and turn your hurts into a harvest to be reaped in the next season!

Moving On to the Next Season

This is the vision you should be focused on in life: *to do whatever it takes to get to the next season God has for you*. That includes assigning your problems to a season. When the devil says, "This is your life," just tell him, "No, Mr. Devil, this is just a season — nothing more!"

> This is the vision you should be focused on in life: *to do whatever it takes to get to the next season God has for you.*

Then it's up to you to start looking to the next season. Get quiet in your heart and listen to what God has to say about it. Repent of anything you have allowed in your life that has kept you stuck in an old season. Then begin to plan for the next season, to declare good things about the next season, to sow for the next season. And *always* obey God immediately when He shows you the next step to take on your way to the future He has for you.

Remember, you're going to have to press into God and cry out to Him for help, for only He is your Deliverer. Don't just cope with that old season — get delivered from it! Let God help you. Let God change you. Let Him change your view so you can learn how to handle difficult situations *His* way and then move on into the next season.

Don't just let problems pile up on you, keeping you stuck in an old season and making you lose your rightful harvest. Make a quality decision to move on; then *do what you have to do to get there*, going after your God-ordained destiny with all your mind, soul, heart, and strength!

GOD BROUGHT US OUT TO BRING US IN

5

*H*as a fire of hope for a better future been ignited in your heart yet? Well, let me "fan the flame" a little further!

You see, you need to know beyond a shadow of a doubt that God doesn't just want to help you escape the undesirable season you've been stuck in for too long. He wants to usher you into a whole new realm of blessing, abundance, and freedom. You can find this principle proclaimed throughout the Bible: *God brings you OUT OF the old so He can bring you INTO the newness of life in Him!*

I want to take you further into the Word and give you a clearer picture of what God has to say about His good plan for your life. You need to *know* these truths, planting them deep in your heart, in order to complete the crucial transition from that old, undesirable season to the next season God has for you.

The Curse Is Reversed!

Let's start by finding out what it really means to be redeemed.

> **Christ has redeemed us from the curse of the law, having become a curse for us (for it is written, "Cursed is everyone who hangs on a tree"),**
> **that the blessing of Abraham might come upon the Gentiles in Christ Jesus, that we might receive the promise of the Spirit through faith.**
>
> **Galatians 3:13,14**

"Christ has redeemed us...." That word "redeemed" has to do with *cutting one's losses.* As we talked about before, it also means *to rescue one from loss; to ransom;* and *to improve one's opportunity.* [16] So if you find yourself in a messy, dead-end situation from which there seems to be no way out, you can rest assured that Jesus, the Anointed One, came to redeem you from that mess — to rescue you from loss and to ransom you in order to improve your opportunity. That's good news, friend! There *is* a way out, and there *are* better days ahead!

Now notice what verse 13 goes on to say: *"Christ has redeemed us from the CURSE...."* Remember, the word "curse" carries the idea of *being hemmed in with obstacles; powerless to resist.* There are a lot of folks in this world who find themselves hemmed in with obstacles and powerless to resist. I call it being stuck in a season! For some people, that cursed condition may be the result of poverty, addiction, perversion, anger, or depression. But whatever the

---

[16] Strong, "Greek Dictionary of the New Testament," #1805.

source of the problem, they all feel the same way — hemmed in by insurmountable obstacles and helpless in their own power to resist.

The good news is this: Jesus came to rescue us from loss and to improve our opportunity so we don't have to stay stuck in old seasons of defeat and failure. *Jesus came to reverse the curse!* He came to set captives free. He came to destroy the works of the devil.

In John 10:10, Jesus said, *"The thief does not come except to steal, and to kill, and to destroy. I have come that they may have life, and that they may have it more abundantly."* The Amplified Bible puts it this way: *"...I came that they may have and enjoy life, and have it in abundance (to the full, till it overflows)."*

Christians are to have *and* enjoy life! Too many people *have* life, but they're not *enjoying* it. Some people are so uptight, bound, and hemmed in by obstacles that they don't see color in their surroundings; they don't taste the flavors of what they eat; and they don't use more than one-eighth of their lungs when they breathe!

We're not supposed to live like that. Jesus said He came so we could have and enjoy life to the full — *until it over-flows.* I want to get over into that place of abundance and *live* there continually, don't you?

But it's important that you understand something: As I heard a minister once say, your *possibility* is not a *positively*. In other words, just because a particular blessing or benefit is possible for you — just because God intends for you to have it and has made a way for you to receive it — doesn't necessarily mean it's automatically going to happen in your life.

Remember, God is not a respecter of *persons*; He is a respecter of *principles*. All the good news found in the Word is for *whosoever will*, not just for a few spiritual elite. However, God's benefits are available to *whosoever will call upon His name*, not whosoever will sit around doing nothing!

It doesn't matter what color your skin is, where you're from, or how tall, pretty, or old you are. It doesn't matter whether you're rich or poor, educated or uneducated. All that matters is that you honor and obey God's principles as set forth in His Word.

> ...God's benefits are available to whosoever will call upon His name, not whosoever will sit around doing nothing!

If you will behave yourself wisely and line yourself up with God's principles, He will rescue you from loss and improve your opportunity. He will deliver you from the obstacles that have hemmed you in for too long and give you all the power you need to resist and overcome every problem or situation you face. It's your choice as one of the redeemed of the Lord!

GOD'S DESTINATION FOR YOU:
YOUR OWN PERSONAL PROMISED LAND

Why did Jesus rescue us from loss and destruction? Deuteronomy 6:23,24 answers this question:

THEN HE BROUGHT US OUT FROM THERE, THAT HE MIGHT BRING US IN, to give us the land of which He swore to our fathers.

And the Lord commanded us to observe all these statutes, to fear the Lord our God, for our good always, that He might preserve us alive, as it is this day.

God brought us out so that He might bring us in. Get ahold of this principle, because it reveals a divine pattern in the way God deals with us. He brings us out of a bad season so that He might bring us into a better season. God *always* has a destination in mind. It is never enough for Him to get us out of a bad situation and leave it at that.

Far too many people have the "just let me out" mentality. These people live their lives just trying to get out of the messy situations they're in at the moment — situations often created by their own lack of self-control. They have no concept of moving toward a new destination. The only destination they have is *out*: "I have to get out from under this pressure. I have to get away from this problem. I have to get these creditors off my back!"

> God *always* has a destination in mind. It is never enough for Him to get us out of a bad situation and leave it at that.

Some have relationship problems with their spouse, their boss, their neighbor, etc. But they're not willing to change themselves to make the relationship better; they just want to get away from the hassle and the pressure of trying to make that troubled relationship work.

My stepfather is a construction superintendent. When he supervises a construction job, he has a lot of men working for him who have this kind of mentality. The men will come on the job and ask my stepfather if he needs any help. The men are good workers, but about eight weeks later after they make enough money to get the creditors off their backs and still have enough left over for food and beer, these construction workers say, "See ya!" and take off! Soon they run out of money and begin to borrow from everyone they can. When that doesn't work anymore, they come back to the construction site, ready to work again.

Even though that kind of life never goes anywhere, a lot of people keep that kind of mindset their entire lives. They just want to get out of their current financial jam so they can go back to living the way they want to live. They say, "I hope that MasterCard I just applied for comes through so I can use it to make my Visa payment, because I used that Visa to pay off my other MasterCard, which I used to pay off my Sears, Penney's, and Texaco cards!"

How do I know about that? Because I've been there! Thank God, I'm out of that season, and I am not going back!

God is a Deliverer, and He has a specific pattern of deliverance. When you call upon Him, He hears you and delivers you. But God wants to bring you out of the tough spots and the undesirable situations for one purpose: so that He can bring you to His destination for your life — your own promised land.

The land spoken of in Deuteronomy 6:23 is not a type of Heaven; rather, it is representative of God's promises, and His promises always reflect what He intends for us. He brings us out that He might bring us in — out of an old season and into a new season, and always for our good.

The Promised Land also represents New Covenant life on this earth. After all, we're not going to face giants in Heaven! There won't be any rogue nations that we have to chase out. The real-life adversaries the Israelites faced in Canaan are representative of our life here on this earth. This is where we have to fight the good fight of faith and overcome the enemy of our souls!

The Promised Land therefore reflects the abundant life that God intends for you to live. Verse 23 also says that God swore to your fathers to give it to you. That means He has intended to give you a future and a hope for a long time. I don't know about you, but I want to be brought out of my undesirable seasons so I can be brought into the promises and intentions that God has had for my life long before I was ever born!

Your Destination Is Not the Wilderness

As believers, we're supposed to be alert and alive — lovers of truth, not just hearers of sermons. If our only destination is *out*, we'll have nowhere to go but to a new set of problems in the next season. As a result, we'll always live our lives in a "recycled crisis" mode as we wander through the wilderness.

I'm telling you, God has a better destination for you than the wilderness! He wants to bring you out of the present crisis so He might bring you into the good plan He has intended for you all along!

If you get out of your mess only to wander in the wilderness, the sun will bake your brain and you'll start talking crazy like the children of Israel did. They decided they wanted to go back to the bondage of Egypt! You'll start thinking and talking the same way: *I'm just going to go back to my old way of thinking, my old friends, and my old lifestyle. At least I had fun back then.* If you start thinking that way, you can know that the sun has baked your brain. You're forgetting too much — and it could cost you your promised land!

That's what happened to an entire generation of Israelites. It was God's intention to bring them out of Egypt in order to bring them into the Promised Land. But although many were brought out, most of that older generation never made it in.

If we want to make sure we don't share the fate of that generation, we need to discover the reasons they didn't enter into their Promised Land as God intended. Hebrews 3:16-19 gives us a clue:

> **For who, having heard, rebelled? Indeed, was it not all who came out of Egypt, led by Moses?**
> **Now with whom was He angry forty years? Was it not with those who sinned, whose corpses fell in the wilderness?**
> **And to whom did He swear that they would not enter His rest, but to those who did not obey?**
> **So we see that they could not enter in because of unbelief.**

This is written as an example to us. The Scriptures tell us that God brought out the children of Israel that He might bring them in, but some of them couldn't enter into what He had intended for them *because of unbelief* and *disobedience*. This is confirmed in Hebrews 4:11 (*AMP*):

> **Let us therefore be zealous and exert ourselves and strive diligently to enter that rest [of God, to know and experience it for ourselves], that no one may fall or perish by the same kind of unbelief and disobedience [into which those in the wilderness fell].**

What will keep you from ever experiencing God's intentions for you? *Unbelief* and *disobedience*. These are the two root causes for the children of Israel being brought out but never making it in. If we're not careful, those same two root causes will also keep us wandering in the desert, stuck in old seasons of bondage and defeat.

A conservative estimate of the time it should have taken for the Israelites to make the trip from Egypt (God bringing them out) to the Promised Land (God bringing them in) is less than two weeks. In addition, the Bible says that no one was feeble among them (Ps. 105:37). Regardless of their age, God supernaturally strengthened His people so they could make the journey.

But through unbelief and disobedience, the children of Israel turned the whole shooting match into a forty-year marathon! And here's the really sad part: Of all those millions of people in that older generation, only two of them made it into the land God had promised them!

Why didn't that generation make it? Didn't God bring them out so He could bring them in? Yes, and He never varied from His original purpose and intention. But although He brought them out, He could not bring them in. In the end, they died in the desert, unable to enter into the land of promise because of their unbelief and disobedience.

The obvious response to the Israelites' example is this: In order to enter into a brighter future and a new season in God, you must both *believe* and *obey*. That may seem very simplistic, but that's the way it works in the Kingdom of God.

> In order to enter into a brighter future and a new season in God, you must both *believe* and *obey*.

Five Manifestations of Disobedience

Personally, I don't want to be brought out of bondage just so I can wander around in the wilderness of life. I want to be brought *out* so that I can be brought *in*. But I also realize that I have a responsibility because of God's call on my life to help others get out of the wilderness. I don't want to give a happy little message to the people within range of my influence about being brought out and being brought in without telling the whole truth.

We have to realize that we have some personal responsibility in this matter. It is fully clear that although God wants to bring us out so that He can bring us in, we must fulfill our part by believing in Him and obeying His Word.

In First Corinthians 10, we find that these two roots of unbelief and disobedience manifested themselves in five specific ways in that older generation of Israelites. The Holy Spirit inspired the apostle Paul to specifically record these manifestations of disobedience as an example and a warning to us. If we will heed His warning, we'll be able to avoid making the same mistakes the Israelites did that kept them out of their Promised Land.

> **Moreover, brethren, I do not want you to be unaware that all our fathers were under the cloud, all passed through the sea,**
> **all were baptized into Moses in the cloud and in the sea,**
> **all ate the same spiritual food,**
> **and all drank the same spiritual drink. For they drank of that spiritual Rock that followed them, and that Rock was Christ.**

But with most of them God was not well pleased, for their bodies were scattered in the wilderness.

Now these things became our examples, to the intent that we should not lust after evil things as they also lusted.

And do not become idolaters as were some of them. As it is written, "The people sat down to eat and drink, and rose up to play."

Nor let us commit sexual immorality, as some of them did, and in one day twenty-three thousand fell;

nor let us tempt Christ, as some of them also tempted, and were destroyed by serpents;

nor complain, as some of them also complained, and were destroyed by the destroyer.

Now all these things happened to them as examples, and they were written for our admonition, upon whom the ends of the ages have come.

Therefore let him who thinks he stands take heed lest he fall.

No temptation has overtaken you except such as is common to man; but God is faithful, who will not allow you to be tempted beyond what you are able, but with the temptation will also make the way of escape, that you may be able to bear it.

1 Corinthians 10:1-13

All the children of Israel went through the same supernatural deliverance from the bondage of Egypt. All of them experienced God's faithfulness, provision, protection, and goodness demonstrated toward them. Nevertheless, most of them did not enter into their next season.

As we study this passage of Scripture, you may find some answers to the questions you've been asking yourself: *Why is it that I can't seem to move into my next season? Why am I never promoted? Why can't I get over to that better place?* God is faithful, powerful, and a Giver of good gifts. His intentions are to bring you out so that He can bring you into what He intends for you. However, you have some responsibility too.

That's why God wants you to pay attention to what happened to the Israelites. As Paul exhorts in verses 11 and 12, *"Now all these things happened to them as examples, and they were written for our admonition, upon whom the ends of the ages have come. Therefore let him who thinks he stands take heed lest he fall."*

Now, I'm not saying that every one of these manifestations will apply to you personally. But I believe that most of them apply to all of us at one time or another in our lives. Therefore, we would all do well to take heed, for every one of these five manifestations of sin end in destruction. Every one of them will prevent us from entering into the next season God has for us.

#I: LUST

Verse 6 tells us that the first manifestation of disobedience is *lust*: *"Now these things became our examples, to the intent that we should not lust after evil things as they also lusted."*

Whenever we mention lust, we immediately think of sexual lust. But lust actually refers to a strong desire or craving for anything. For instance, we can lust for chocolate chip cookies!

Suppose you see a commercial about fresh chocolate chip cookies, and your mind gets distracted by the thought of eating those cookies. Or you walk by a bakery where fresh chocolate chip cookies are being baked, and you immediately do a "u-turn." You decide you just can't be happy until you eat a whole batch of chocolate chip cookies! That's an example of a strong craving, a distracting desire, a lust after wrong things — or in this case, too much of a good thing!

Lust is a manifestation of disobedience that will keep us from entering into our promised land. It means that even though we are born again, we are being carnal, living after the flesh. Wanting our own way, we crave things we know are wrong. More often than not, this kind of strong desire for evil things is fueled by those we hang out with.

Numbers 11:4 (*AMP*) talks about the danger of associating closely with the wrong people:

> **And the mixed multitude among them [the rabble who followed Israel from Egypt] began to lust greatly [for familiar and dainty food], and the Israelites wept again and said, Who will give us meat to eat?**

The phrase "mixed multitude" refers to a group of people who were serving a number of different gods. This "rabble" influenced the rest of the Israelites to lust after the delicacies they couldn't have out in the desert, such as meat. But after God gave them more meat than they could ever eat, the children of Israel wished they had stopped complaining before they got what they asked for!

What about you? Do you have people around you who are influencing you the wrong way? The Bible warns, *"Do not be misled. Bad company corrupts good character"* (1 Cor. 15:33 *NIV*). But this can be such a subtle process that you may not even be aware that it is happening.

Your friends may talk about certain things they have done or heard that you know is wrong. But because you want their approval, you find yourself lusting after the same things they do, even though you know you are headed way off course. As you keep associating with these friends, they eventually become more important to you than staying on course with God. You start participating in activities you know are wrong. Finally, you realize that you are once more in bondage and that your downward spiral was fueled by the people you chose to hang out with.

It's okay for Christians to have friends and to be a friend, but they can't walk intimately with God if they place their friendships above their desire to please Him and start lusting after the things of the world. In fact, the Bible warns that if a person hangs out with a fool, he will become a fool and receive a fool's reward (Prov. 13:20). Nevertheless, some people are so insecure that they'd sacrifice anything to have their friends' approval, including their close fellowship with God.

In this modern age, there is one more huge influence on our lives that tempts us to lust: *the media*. So let me ask you this: What are you allowing to influence your life? What movies are you watching? What are you reading? What sites are you visiting on the Internet?

> Don't let the lust for wrong things keep you from your land of promise!

If you can't handle the television or the computer, throw them out in the street. If anything isn't a blessing or a help to you — if it's just a distraction that brings pollution into your life — be man or woman enough to eliminate it from your life. Don't let the lust for wrong things keep you from your land of promise!

#2: IDOLATRY

First Corinthians 10:7 reveals the second manifestation of disobedience: *idolatry.*

> **And do not become idolaters as were some of them. As it is written, "The people sat down to eat and drink, and rose up to play."**

You may think you're safe if you don't know what an idolater is, but you're not. You see, idolatry refers to *any* value system you create that makes anything of more value than God — and it always results in the things of God becoming optional in your life.

- *The Word* becomes optional.
- *Church attendance* becomes optional.
- *Prayer time* becomes optional.
- *Tithing* becomes optional.
- *Serving God* becomes optional.
- *Behaving like a Christian* during the week becomes optional.

This doesn't mean the things we value most are necessarily wrong in themselves; it just means they have become misplaced in our lives. Whenever we value a hobby, a certain kind of food, a dream, a desire, or a goal more than we value our relationship with God, that endeavor will be doomed. We can't put anything ahead of God and expect it to stand.

This kind of error puts us on very dangerous territory. In fact, it can even lead us down a path that becomes deadly. First, we start putting things ahead of God; then the things of God become very optional. Finally, we begin to turn away from pursuing our walk with God, whether openly or secretly, consciously or unconsciously. In the end, we lose out on the next season God has for us and the good future He intends for us to enjoy.

You know, we live in a very serious day. There are people in this world who are so crazed and warped on their own, they don't even need the devil to make them that way! As a result, the amount of money we spend as a nation on security has risen considerably. For instance, almost 320 million dollars was spent on security for the eighteen days of the 2002 Winter Olympic games in Utah! We are definitely taking national security more seriously than we ever have before!

So many things are taken seriously in this day, yet so many Christians still don't take the things of God seriously. They maintain a "let's play" attitude, treating lightly that which is holy and sacred.

As parents, we sometimes get after our children about putting their toys away. We might tell them that they can't come inside until they have picked up the balls, skateboards, dolls, wagons, and other toys that are littered all over the yard.

Yet we live our spiritual lives with the same casual mindset we're trying to train our children *not* to have! We spend most of our time and energy on natural pursuits; meanwhile, half the time we're not even sure where we last saw our Bible!

You need to be very careful that this doesn't describe *your* life. Don't allow even a hint of idolatry to touch your life. Why? Because the moment the things of God become optional to you is the moment you will take yourself off the path that leads to your next season in God's good plan.

#3: SEXUAL IMPURITY

Verse 8 gives us the third manifestation of disobedience —
sexual sin.

Nor let us commit sexual immorality, as some of them did, and in one day twenty-three thousand fell.

This manifestation has to do with impurity and with accepting an ungodly standard of modesty and behavior. It has to do with what you watch, what you wear, how you wear what you wear, and how you behave when you wear it.

Don't misunderstand me — I'm not saying that as Christians, we need to dress up in burlap bags! I believe that men and women of God need to look good and dress sharply. Women can look gorgeous. Men can look classy. Christians should make an effort to clothe and to carry themselves as the redeemed of the Most High.

I'm not trying to make us all into prudes; I'm just saying we are not to buy into the world's system. We need to stay out of extremes on either side of this issue. This might sound a little strong, but the common perception in society is that what we're willing to show, we're willing to share. Therefore, we need to be very careful in the way we present ourselves to the outside world.

I have a teenage daughter who is beautiful. As a father, I'm not sure I like that! When we go into restaurants and I see grown men looking at her, my wife has to remind me to put down the steak knife!

A couple of years ago my daughter innocently mailed in a card that offered a sample copy of a teenage magazine for girls. I looked at the magazine when it came to our house.

It talked about how to kiss, how to be sexy, and who all the sexy boy groups were. I knew I didn't want that garbage delivered to my daughter, so my wife called the company and told them not to send any more copies of the magazine.

Some people think they have to be friends to their children, allowing them to do "what everyone else is doing" in order to make them happy. But the best way parents can be friends to their children is by loving them enough to draw some godly boundaries for their lives!

In Sweden, it is against the law in that country for parents to even discipline their children — to spank them or to touch them in any corrective way. As a result, the Swedish society is dealing with a generation of young people who are as free as kites, but they don't feel loved. Significantly, Sweden has the highest teenage suicide rate in the world.

As Christians, we need to come back to purity and not allow the world to tell us how to dress and talk. We need to behave properly and modestly toward one another. The world may talk crudely, but that doesn't mean we have to. People in the world may want to "show their stuff," but we don't have to look at them or allow those images to come into our homes through the media. We have to draw some lines in our lives according to God's Word!

Personally, I've made the decision to draw lines for me and mine and for this ministry. But I can't come into your house and draw lines; that's *your* responsibility.

The only way we can live in the fullness of God's plan for us is to draw some lines in our lives regarding purity. If we take on the ways and the thoughts of the world, we'll never be able to enter our own personal land of promise as God intends.

If you have allowed *any* form of sexual impurity in your life, you need to deal with it immediately and get it under the blood of Jesus. Make it a non-issue in your life so that nothing hinders you from leaving the wilderness of that old season once and for all. Get your eyes off what the world has to offer, and fix your gaze on the new season that's just waiting for you!

#4: TEMPTING CHRIST

First Corinthians 10:9 warns us of the fourth manifestation of disobedience to avoid in our lives:

> **Nor let us tempt Christ, as some of them also tempted, and were destroyed by serpents.**

"To tempt" means *to test fully.*[17] One translation says we are not to "go too far in testing the Lord's patience."[18] In other words, we are not to try God to see how far He will let us go in sin, disregarding how He feels about our disobedience until it finally costs us.

This verse is a wake-up call to all of us. We are not to live the way we want to live, thinking there will be no consequences. God is not our substitute teacher!

I remember the grief that I and my classmates would give to any substitute teacher we had in band class. We always tried to see how far we could go before we got in

---

[17] Ibid., #1598.

[18] William F. Beck, *The New Testament in the Language of Today* as quoted in *The Bible From 26 Translations*, Curtis Vaughn, Th.D., ed., (Moss Point, MS: Baker Book House by Mathis Publishers, Inc., 1988), p. 2302.

trouble. We'd switch instruments so that clarinet players would be sitting in the flute section and flute players would be sitting in the trumpet section. We'd go as far as we could go before it cost us.

There are a lot of Christians who live that way, counting on the fact that God is merciful. Yes, God is merciful, but remember — we're not talking about how we can make Heaven by the skin of our teeth. We're talking about our responsibility to cooperate with God so that not only can we be brought *out of* the kingdom of darkness, but also brought *into* the fullness of God's plan for our lives.

We are deceiving ourselves if we think we can continue to allow sin in our lives without suffering any consequences. That's what the devil tried to tell Eve. She told the serpent she couldn't eat of that tree, but the serpent told her that it really didn't matter — she wouldn't die. But Eve found out very quickly that disobedience does matter very much to God!

> We are deceiving ourselves if we think we can continue to allow sin in our lives without suffering any consequences.

We have to get our thoughts and our ways lined up with the thoughts and the ways of God. Time is too short to keep running into walls, yet that is exactly what will happen if we refuse to stop tempting God with our disobedience.

Do you know what I mean by "running into a wall"? Consider the role of an outfielder in professional baseball. He stands in position on the green grass. When a long fly ball comes his way, he starts running on that grass toward the back wall, keeping his eyes on the ball at all times.

In front of the wall is a warning track made of dirt that enables the outfielder to know he is getting close to the wall without having to look. At that moment, he has to make a decision: He can either let the ball go, or he can run into the wall in an effort to catch it.

Too many Christians spend their lives running into walls because they continually ignore "the warning track" God has set in front of them. They just keep running, thinking that a little sin doesn't matter. Sure, it's wrong, but it's the way they want to live. *God is merciful,* they think. *He'll forgive me.* So relying on "sloppy grace" and ignoring the warning track, they keep on running — straight into the wall that looms up ahead.

But these are the last days, and time is very short. We're running out of warning track. We have to stop hitting the wall so we can take our God-ordained place in this end-time season of His purposes.

#5: MURMURING

Finally, verse 10 gives us the fifth manifestation of disobedience:

> **Nor complain, as some of them also complained, and were destroyed by the destroyer.**

To murmur means *to grumble and complain in low tones.* It occurs where dissatisfaction, discontent, and rebellion are present, and it reveals a person's lack of belief in God's goodness, ability, and knowledge.

I don't believe that born-again, Spirit-filled, blood-bought people should be complainers. I don't think they should be the ones lined up at the service counter in the store, banging their fists on the counter and getting all worked up about an defective item! Christians who act like that are a big reason why a lot of people aren't Christians themselves!

If we have business to take care of, there is a godly way to do it. Instead of being murmurers and complainers, we need to be gracious, kind, and honorable toward other people. When we call people by their name and treat them with a little respect, favor will be released toward us.

First Corinthians 10:9 talks about Israelites who actually dropped dead because they refused to stop murmuring. They were even complaining about the food and the drink God supernaturally provided for them! God's provision and goodness in their lives just wasn't enough for them — yet they were voicing their complaints with the very breath that God had given them! If I were God, I'd have withheld those people's next breath until they decided to stop complaining. From what the Bible tells us about these Israelites, there would have been a lot of blue-faced people!

We must be careful that we are not complainers and that we don't allow discontent in our lives. In Philippians 4:11 and 13, Paul said, "...*I have learned in whatever state I am, to be content.... I can do all things through Christ who strengthens me.*" Paul knew who his Source was and lived accordingly. We need to do the same.

CHECK UP ON YOURSELF

How should you respond to this study of the five manifestations of disobedience? First, you need to get your target right. The target is *you*. You need to apply these divine warnings to your own life, not to other people.

However, you need to make sure that you don't try to apply this passage of Scripture to what is already under the blood of Jesus. That's not what we're talking about here. If you already asked forgiveness for past sins, God has forgotten them; those sins can't even be found in His heart and mind any longer! I don't care if you used to be "a joker, a smoker, and a midnight toker"! If that's what you used to be, leave that which is in your past in your past. Don't dishonor the blood of Jesus by bringing up what has already been cleansed.

We're talking about your *present* season. Where are you at now? Check up on yourself, and if you recognize any manifestations of disobedience that you may be allowing in your life, get it under the blood through repentance and move on!

God wants to bring His people out so He can bring them in. But the way some Christians are living in this day and age, they're like a person who tries to board an airplane without a ticket, wearing no shoes or socks, and dragging a lawnmower behind him! While that person is wondering where his seat is, the stewardess is trying to tell him that he can't get on the plane that way!

Similarly, you aren't going to be able to "board the plane" of your next season while you're still dragging excess baggage of unbelief and disobedience — *especially* in these last days when time is so short. You're going to have to change some things, friend. God is calling you to lay down whatever is keeping you stuck in old seasons of loss, failure, and lack.

How do you begin that process of change? It all comes back to the Word of God. You see, you won't know what to trust, who to believe, or what to obey without God's Word. This is the reason you must have daily exposure to and intake of the Word. As Romans 10:17 says, *"…faith comes by hearing, and hearing by the word of God."* As you feed your spirit with the Word on a daily basis, you'll begin to see what God wants you to do, and you'll realize that His commandments are always for your own good.

Certainly that is true regarding this passage in First Corinthians 10. These verses were written for our instruction, as both an example and a warning. They present a message of divine love, not of condemnation. God wants us to check up on ourselves because He wants us to be able to enter into what He intends for us. He loves us enough to interrupt our lives and announce that He brought us *out* in order to bring us *in* — and that He *can't* bring us in as long as disobedience and unbelief remain in our lives.

David understood the importance of checking up on himself in his personal walk with God. In Psalm 139, David wrote:

> **Search me, O God, and know my heart; test me and know my anxious thoughts.**
> **See if there is any offensive way in me, and lead me in the way everlasting.**
>
> **Psalm 139:23,24 NIV**

After we examine ourselves, we need to repent of anything we find in our lives that is displeasing to God. We can see this principle in the apostle Peter's sermon to the multitudes, where he proclaimed not only our need for repentance, but the blessings that will inevitably follow:

> **So repent (change your mind and purpose); turn around and return [to God], that your sins may be erased (blotted out, wiped clean), that times of refreshing (of recovering from the effects of heat, of reviving with fresh air) may come from the presence of the Lord.**
>
> **Acts 3:19** *AMP*

God is asking you to look on the inside and to lay some things down. He isn't condemning you; He is endeavoring to help you get "unstuck." He is making sure you don't fall in the wilderness, never experiencing the abundance and joy of His good plan for your life. God just wants you to get rid of every manifestation of disobedience in your life so you can "board the plane" and enter into all that He has for you!

So take the time to search your heart. Determine on the inside that none of these hindrances are worth holding on to, for in the end they will only keep you out of the fullness of God's plan for your life.

Then do what the Bible says to do: *Repent.* Just stop going in that direction; turn around; and return to God. Speak to every "mountain" and tell it to leave your life in the Name of Jesus. Then turn to God and say, "Lord, help me." God will forgive you. He'll erase your sins, and you will be made clean by the blood of Jesus.

From that moment on, you'll have a fresh start — as long as you stay keen and sharp in your walk with Him. If those strongholds try to resurface, the Lord will help you resist their pull. And as you depend on His power to give you strength in your inner man, you will walk into the next season *free* of every weight and sinful hindrance!

MAKE A *DECISION*

As we deal with any areas of disobedience or unbelief that may be keeping us out of our land of promise, there is a powerful combination of spiritual principles we need to embrace and put into action in our lives. These principles will not only help us kick down the doors of the old season; they will also keep us going until we have reached the new season God has for us. The combination I'm talking about has two crucial components: *decisions* and *declarations*.

Your first step is to make a quality decision to come out of a season. This means you must make a decision for *transformation*, not just for *self-improvement*.

A lot of people like to live according to what amounts to "no-fault" religion. In other words, no matter what happens, they want to be able to say, "It's no fault of mine." They'll blame God, the devil, their pastor, their spouse — anyone but themselves.

But the truth is, if we're not satisfied with the way our lives are going, we need to admit that it's probably our fault. We are the ones who decide what to do with our lives. Therefore, if we want to change the direction we're headed in life, we will have to make some life-changing decisions. We can't keep doing things the way we've always done them and expect problems to just clear up on their own!

For instance, you can't remain your tired, old, grumpy self and expect joy to come back in your relationships. And if you're wanting to lose weight, you can't keep your membership in the "Twinkie of the Month Club"! You'll have to make some changes in your eating and exercise habits if you want to change the way your body looks. You're certainly not going to wake up one morning and all of a sudden be at your ideal body weight!

The same thing is true if you're in debt and are facing substantial financial challenges. You can't keep up the same spending patterns that got you in debt and still expect to catch up! You also can't catch up by playing the lottery instead of looking for a job!

That's what a lot of people try to do. They play the lottery because they don't want to change their spending habits. They want to be rich, but they don't want to work for it. But it just doesn't happen that way in this world.

The only way you'll see change in any area of your life is by making a quality decision to allow God to transform you from the inside out so you can get out of the season you're in.

Some people just keep waiting year after year for something to change in their lives, but they never make a quality decision to leave the season they're in. They may think they have to do something first or get things in order first. They may even be unsure whether they are allowed to leave the undesirable season they've been stuck in for so long.

Let me tell you, friend — you are free to go! Jesus paid the price to deliver you out of that old season. God is bringing you out so He can bring you in! You just have to make the decision to do what you have to do to get going!

A lot of times people put conditions on their ability to leave the bad seasons of their lives. Other people wait because they're unsure whether or not they can really step out and do it. Will they really be able to follow through on their decision and accomplish their goal? That kind of uncertainty often stems from something in people's past. There may have been other times when they tried to step out and do something and nothing happened.

But that mentality is a dangerous one. You will get nowhere in life if you think you can't do something just because it didn't work before. You have to just try again. In fact, don't *try* — just *do* it! But this time, make sure you say this from your heart: "God, help me. Lord, change me. Anything You tell me to do, I'll do, Lord. And as I obey You, I'll expect Heaven to back me up. I'll expect You to bring some 'super' upon my 'natural' to help me finish this course!"

If you wait for all the conditions to be favorable before you ever start moving out of your present season, you'll never do anything in life. It is a matter of knowing on the inside that you have the counsel of God and the peace of the Holy Ghost. Then with firm resolve, you make the decision that you *are* moving on to a new and better season.

Life is not a flip of the coin. *You* are the one who determines the outcome. Let me put it to you this way: If you are given an umbrella, and you stand under that umbrella when it's raining, you'll stay dry. But what happens if you move out from under that umbrella while it's still raining? You'll get wet! Was it the umbrella's choice that you got wet? No, it was *your* choice. You chose wet instead of dry.

> Life is not a flip of the coin. *You* are the one who determines the outcome.

The principle is this: *You position yourself by your decisions.* You choose whether you are going to be blessed or not blessed in this life. This is confirmed in Deuteronomy 30:19,20:

> **"I call heaven and earth as witnesses today against you, that I have set before you life and death, blessing and cursing; therefore choose life, that both you and your descendants may live;**
>
> **that you may love the Lord your God, that you may obey His voice, and that you may cling to Him, for He is your life and the length of your days; and that you may dwell in the land which the Lord swore to your fathers, to Abraham, Isaac, and Jacob, to give them."**

Here is another point to understand: *Decisions translate into energy.* Nothing happens until you make a decision. A graphic illustration of this principle can be seen in the process of a wife getting ready for church. If a husband sees his wife pacing back and forth in front of her closet, saying, "I don't know what to wear," he can know that his wife will not be getting dressed until she makes a decision! She might rifle through her clothes in the closet; she might even try on this dress or that outfit. But she'll never be ready to go to church until she makes a decision.

Your quality decision to get out of your old season will be the energy you need to help you move on. Otherwise, you will find yourself in the unenviable position of just coping — trapped in the "going-nowhere" attitude that says, "Well, such is my life." No, you need to make the decision, "This is *not* my life! It's nothing more than a season, and I'm coming out of it, starting today!"

You do what you decide to do. That principle can work both positively and negatively in your life. If some important things don't get done in your life, there is ultimately one reason: You decided not to do what you needed to do.

Some people try to say they can't do anything about the negative things that are happening in their lives. But they *can* decide to do something about it. Their lives may be out of control right now; they may even be at the point where most onlookers would say they *can't* help it. But the truth is, those people made some decisions along the way that helped put them in their present mess. The good news is this: They can now begin to make quality decisions that will move them out of that messy situation for good!

Of course, you may face a lot of opposition when you change course and start making good decisions for your life. For instance, suppose you never earned a college degree, so you decide to go back to college in your middle-age years. The moment you make that decision, you immediately begin to hear from all kinds of naysayers who want to tell you all the reasons it will never work.

But remember — *you will do what you decide to do.* So if you make a quality decision to finish college and get a degree, you *will* get it done, no matter what anyone else says!

What do I mean by a "quality decision"? I'm talking about *a decision you make about which there is no argument or further discussion and from which there is no retreat* — even though you will be tempted to do both.

We live in a day where everyone retreats from their commitments. Escape clauses are included in contracts of every kind; prenuptial agreements are now the rule instead of the exception. A person can even get out of the Army if he wants to!

But you can't have that kind of mindset if you want to experience God's highest in life. *You have to make a quality decision to move on.* Decisions translate into energy and transform apathy into action. Decisions also set your course and determine your destination.

If you want to succeed in flowing from one season to the next in God's plan for your life, you can't just wander around, waiting to "see how it goes." You are not to live your life according to "how it goes"! At some point, you have to put your hand to the plow and *make the decision to do something!*

"The bridge is out. Well, that's all right — I can swim! But it isn't water; it's acid. All right then, I'll jump! One way or another, I'm going to get to my destination!"

That's the kind of resolve you have to build on the inside of yourself. When you make that kind of quality decision to move forward in God's plan for you, Heaven will surely back you up! God will move on your behalf, giving you divine assistance in your time of need.

MAKE A *DECLARATION*

Hebrews 11:3 says, *"By faith we understand that the worlds were framed by the word of God...."* This scripture reveals that *words frame worlds.* The world you live in has been framed and formed by words — words that both you and others have spoken and that you have made a part of your life.

Words are absolutely vital. In fact, the Bible says that words contain the power of life and of death (Prov. 18:21). Words either free you, or they bind you. Words either build you up, or they tear you down. Words either encourage you and cheer you on, or they discourage you and defeat you.

Therefore, you have to be careful about the kind of words you speak, as well as the words you hear others speak about you. After all, your decisions, which are formed out of words, determine not only the framework of your world, but the ultimate outcome of your life!

This brings us to the second principle in the powerful combination that, when acted upon, will propel you into the new season God has for you. After you have made that quality *decision* to get out of the old season, it takes a *declaration* to start moving toward the new one. A declaration has to do with something you declare or say from your heart. It is burned into the hallways of your inner being. It is something on the inside of you that you proclaim with full intention and resolve.

Your declaration both enforces and reinforces your decisions. Therefore, once you decide to come out of your old season, you need to declare that decision with the words of your mouth.

It doesn't matter if you have been broke, depressed, or sick. At some point, you have to decide to grab hold of the rim of that miry pit, pull yourself up, and declare, *"I'm coming out of here!"* You *decide*, and then you *make a declaration*. That declaration will not only get you going, but it will *keep* you going as well. It will not only *enforce* that decision, but it will *reinforce* it in the days ahead when you are tempted to give up and quit.

These two spiritual principles apply to every area of life. Before you can change direction or cause something good to happen in a proactive way, you must first decide something, and then you must declare it to be so. This is exactly what Job 22:28 (*AMP*) is talking about:

> **You shall also decide and decree a thing, and it shall be established for you; and the light [of God's favor] shall shine upon your ways.**

When you decide and decree something, it *will* be established in your life. The truth is, *nothing* happens until you declare it. Jesus is not Lord until you declare Jesus as Lord. Life just works that way.

This truth is powerful when you learn to direct it correctly, put faith behind it, and cause it to go in a positive direction. That's when God can put His resources behind your words! On the other hand, if you wake up tomorrow and say with grumpy conviction, "This is going to be a cruddy day," guess what? You will have a cruddy day! You decided it; you decreed it; and your faith was released for it. Therefore, you received what you established with your words.

> When you decide and decree something, it *will* be established in your life.

When I perform a wedding, I try to tie a good knot so the bride and groom can't unravel it. They stand before me, and near the end of the ceremony I say, "I now pronounce you husband and wife." Before that moment, those two people made a *decision* to become husband and wife, but their union doesn't happen until the moment I *declare* that they are husband and wife. Of course, at that moment, the life they will experience together as husband and wife still hasn't taken place yet. *But as with everything else in life, marriage begins with a declaration.* At that moment, they are no longer two; they have become one flesh in the eyes of God.

Let's take another example from life in this natural world. Suppose a real estate agent shows a house to a prospective buyer. As they walk through the house, the buyer starts to envision the way he would furnish and decorate it. However, it isn't the buyer's house until he decides to buy it; makes a declaration to the real estate agent that he will buy it; and then does something about his decision.

The moment the buyer signs his name on the dotted line, he can declare that the house is his. That doesn't mean all his furnishings and decorations are automatically in place. His knickknacks are not yet hung up on the walls, and his scented candles are not yet burning. Settling into a new home takes time — but it all begins with a *decision* and a *declaration*.

The words you hear about yourself and the words you speak all help to form your decisions, and it is your decisions that lead to your declarations. This is very important to understand, because you can make this powerful principle work for you to help you get to the next season. Just begin to declare from this moment forward, "I'm out of this old season! Devil, I can't hear you, because I'm not listening anymore! I'm entering right now into the new season God has for me!"

Don't just think those words — *you need to open your mouth and speak them*. That doesn't mean you need to go stand by the big fountain in the mall and shout so everyone can hear you. Your declaration isn't for them — it's for your God; it's for a defeated devil; and it's for those around you of like precious faith. But more than anything, it is for *you*.

Launched out of your own spirit man, your declaration of faith is immediately caught right back by your spirit to help you hold fast in the midst of the storm. That which you decree will be established in your life, so continually declare by faith: "I am well able to overcome this situation! Just as God delivered David from the paw of the lion and the bear and from the hand of the Philistine, God will deliver *me*. And He is not only bringing me *out* — He is bringing me *into* the land of promise. God has been wanting this for me for a long time, so right now I leave my old season, and I step into my future and my hope. I am in a new season now!"

The moment you make that declaration, something has changed. The scenery may not have changed yet, but you are *now* in your new season. Even though you can't see it yet, you can know you've come through the gate — because everything begins with a declaration!

Remember, you are to walk by faith, not by sight (2 Cor. 5:7). It is what you trust in but do not yet see that will keep you going.

I see a natural example of this principle every year when I plant new seeds in my backyard garden. I'll plant the seeds in the spring after the danger of frost has passed. Once I'm finished planting the seeds, I can truthfully say I have a garden, even though when I look at it, I only see dirt, posts, and strings. Am I eating out of my garden yet? No, not yet. Do I have anything to show for it yet? No. But I know that even though the scenery hasn't yet changed, something hidden is happening that will soon bring forth visible fruit. And I guarantee you that the first time I see the smallest green sprout popping through the dirt, I will rejoice!

In the same way, every time you declare by faith that you are in a new season, your words are plowing, planting, and watering the garden of your life. Certainly there is much more to see and to do. Yes, you still have to walk out the fulfillment of your declaration. But even though you may not see signs of that new season yet, you will. *It's coming.*

So the moment you see those first little green sprouts of victory popping out of the soil, start rejoicing and *keep declaring*! As you do, you'll eventually receive the full harvest of God's blessings that have been waiting for you all along in the next season of your life!

LEARN HOW TO *RELEASE*

I want to talk to you about one more combination of key principles that will help launch you out of an undesirable season and into the next season God has for you: You must first *release* and then *reach*.

Just think for a moment about Tarzan swinging from vine to vine. If Tarzan releases but fails to reach, he falls and gets hurt. But if Tarzan doesn't release and then reaches, he gets hung up between two vines! The same principle applies to our lives in God. If we don't want to fall flat on our faces or get hung up in a bad season, we have to learn to both release *and* reach.

First, let's talk about what you have to do to release certain things in your life. Part of releasing has to do with *forgetting the past.* Look at what Paul said in Philippians 3:13,14:

> Brethren, I do not count myself to have appre-
> hended; but one thing I do, FORGETTING those things
> which are behind and REACHING FORWARD to those
> things which are ahead,
> I press toward the goal for the prize of the upward
> call of God in Christ Jesus.

We need to *release,* or put out of our minds, those things that need to be left in the past and then *reach out* toward that which is ahead of us.

You may ask, "How do I do that? How do I forget what is behind?" Don't let yourself dwell on past hurts, offenses, or disappointments. Don't talk about them or replay them in your mind. I didn't say it would be easy to do this, but you *can* stop thinking and talking about these negative things that only hinder your progress in life.

The reason you assume you can't stop thinking about it is that you keep declaring you can't do it. You have to declare that you *can* stop thinking negative thoughts. Instead of saying, "I can't help but think of those things," declare this: *"My mind is my mind. My mouth is my mouth!"* You *can* help it. You can think and talk about what you *want* to think and talk about!

If you have a thought you don't want, replace it with a bigger and better thought. The Bible calls this *renewing your mind.* Let your mind dwell on good things (Phil. 4:8). Bring your thoughts into captivity to the obedience of Christ (2 Cor. 10:5).

You may be failing in your efforts to forget your past hurts, disappointments, problems, and failures because you won't stop recalling those bad memories to your mind. It may not be possible to completely eradicate those things

179

from your memory, but you *can* put them out of your mind and refuse to keep bringing them up. When a negative thought about the past tries to invade your mind, just kick it out in the Name of Jesus and replace it with a promise from God's Word! Don't let your mind dwell on *anything* from the past that might hinder your progress toward your future.

Releasing also includes your need to *forgive*. You have to let go of any past hurts and offenses caused by other people who wronged you. You also have to let go of your own past failures and mistakes. You have to release all these things through the power of forgiveness.

> Don't let your mind dwell on *anything* from the past that might hinder your progress toward your future.

Some people hold tightly to past hurts and offenses, dragging them from one season to the next like a big ball and chain. Meanwhile, their bitterness grows deeper and stronger, coming out of their mouth and showing up on their faces — until eventually the ball and chain gets too big to budge! Once that happens, these people will never be able to move on to a new season until they finally decide to forgive and to release the offenses they've held on to for so long.

You never have to stay in that kind of bondage. If there are things in your life that need to be forgotten or forgiven, *demand* your release from them. Notify the devil and your circumstances that you're not asking permission to leave — you are demanding to be let go! Your ransom has already been paid by the blood of Jesus!

He has delivered us from the power of darkness and conveyed us into the kingdom of the Son of His love,
   in whom we have redemption through His blood, the forgiveness of sins.

Colossians 1:13,14

This scripture is telling you that the power in the blood of Jesus has set you free from anything and everything, including those negative things from the past! Nothing has power or dominion or sway to hold you back any longer, so turn around and *leave* that ball and chain in the old season once and for all. And should your hand try to grab hold of it on your way out the door, slap your offending hand and *let go* of that thing so you can come on over to your new season!

REACH FORWARD INTO A BETTER FUTURE!

You need to refuse to see the place you're at right now in life as your limit. Perhaps it's your health that is giving you a problem. Don't accept ill health as your life.

I know several people healed in our congregation who were told that their condition was incurable and that they'd be that way for the rest of their lives. But guess what? That *isn't* the way they are today. They decided to release their disease and reach forward by faith for a new season of divine health!

> ...Refuse to see the place you're at right now in life as your limit.

If you've had financial setbacks in the past, don't let those setbacks be your limit. Yes, you could choose to stay

181

in your situation of financial struggle and just cope. Or you could spend all your time licking your wounds or moaning and groaning about how bad that setback was. But if you do any of these things, you'll just end up stuck in a season. As I said earlier, I don't believe you are called to cope — you are called to *be delivered*. You have to release the financial setbacks in your past and reach forward for the future of abundance and blessing that God has planned for you.

If you truly want "the prize of the upward call of God in Christ Jesus," you will have to stretch beyond the pain and the negative circumstances that still surround you and reach *into* your future and your hope. I'm talking about a *long* reach of faith — so long that there is no turning back once you've decided to commit to it.

I like to watch the Winter Olympics, and my favorite event is the ski jump. In previous years when I traveled to Sweden and Canada, I was able to tour some previous Olympic sites, and I saw the huge ski jump ramps that are built for the event.

When a skier takes his turn at the event, he eases out and sits on a pole. Then he grabs hold of another pole and starts to rock. When the buzzer goes off, he reaches out, grabs hold, pulls himself through the gate, and starts skiing down that steep ramp. From the moment he starts down that ramp, he's at the point of no return! He certainly doesn't have any brakes or turn signals in case he changes his mind!

After jumping off the end of the ramp, that Olympic skier seems to glide through the air as he reaches forward with his entire body, trying to gain as much distance as possible before he lands. That's the kind of long reach I'm talking about — the kind we need to make in the realm of the Spirit in order to move higher in God!

We can't just stay in the warm little hut at the top of the hill. It's time to reach out and pull ourselves through the gate! And from that moment on, we should never entertain another thought about going backwards in our walk with God. When we are reaching out the way God wants us to, there *is* no return — just a leap forward into a better, more fulfilling future!

STAY ON GUARD AS YOU
PRESS TOWARD THE GOAL

Paul gave us a better understanding of the nature of that long reach in Philippians 3:14 when he said he was *pressing toward* the goal. "To press" means *to strain and stretch.* You have to *strain* and *stretch* for what is ahead. After all, if it was easy to attain, you'd already have it! You have to *work* at it — and in the midst of your diligent effort to move forward, you have to stay on guard so the enemy can't steal the ground you've already gained.

We see this principle demonstrated in the book of Nehemiah. The children of Israel had been in captivity for many years, and Nehemiah's position in captivity was to be the cupbearer for the king.

One day Nehemiah received word that Jerusalem, the heart of his people's culture and history, had been destroyed and was lying in ruins — the walls broken down and the gates burned with fire. When Nehemiah heard this news, he was deeply grieved. Knowing that God is a covenant-making, covenant-keeping God, Nehemiah prayed, asking for favor with the king so he might be allowed to return with other Jews to Jerusalem in order to rebuild it. In Nehemiah 2:1-6 (*NIV*), Nehemiah himself tells what happened next:

> In the month of Nisan in the twentieth year of King Artaxerxes, when wine was brought for him, I took the wine and gave it to the king. I had not been sad in his presence before;
>
> so the king asked me, "Why does your face look so sad when you are not ill? This can be nothing but sadness of heart." I was very much afraid,
>
> but I said to the king, "May the king live forever! Why should my face not look sad when the city where my fathers are buried lies in ruins, and its gates have been destroyed by fire?"
>
> The king said to me, "What is it you want?" Then I prayed to the God of heaven,
>
> and I answered the king, "If it pleases the king and if your servant has found favor in his sight, let him send me to the city in Judah where my fathers are buried so that I can rebuild it."
>
> Then the king, with the queen sitting beside him, asked me, "How long will your journey take, and when will you get back?" It pleased the king to send me; so I set a time.

Then Nehemiah asked the king if he would write a royal letter allowing him to pass through all the nations to get to Jerusalem. Nehemiah also asked for a letter addressed to those in charge of the timber so he could get all the timber he needed to rebuild. The king kept agreeing to Nehemiah's requests because the gracious hand of God was upon this righteous man (v. 8). The king even offered to send captains and horsemen with Nehemiah as well.

Nehemiah left with everything the king gave him. Arriving at Jerusalem, Nehemiah's heart was crushed by the devastation he saw. Nevertheless, the people had a heart to work, so he began to rally them together and get them started in the rebuilding process.

However, the people weren't just faced with the massive task of rebuilding; they also had to deal with enemies who didn't want to see Jerusalem get rebuilt. These enemies first came to ridicule the people as they worked, trying to discourage and confuse them. Then the enemy started resorting to threats:

> But when Sanballat, Tobiah, the Arabs, the Ammonites and the men of Ashdod heard that the repairs to Jerusalem's walls had gone ahead and that the gaps were being closed, they were very angry.
>
> They all plotted together to come and fight against Jerusalem and stir up trouble against it.
>
> But we prayed to our God and posted a guard day and night to meet this threat.
>
> Meanwhile, the people in Judah said, "The strength of the laborers is giving out, and there is so much rubble that we cannot rebuild the wall."
>
> Also our enemies said, "Before they know it or see us, we will be right there among them and will kill them and put an end to the work."
>
> Then the Jews who lived near them came and told us ten times over, "Wherever you turn, they will attack us."
>
> Therefore I stationed some of the people behind the lowest points of the wall at the exposed places, posting them by families, with their swords, spears and bows.
>
> After I looked things over, I stood up and said to the nobles, the officials and the rest of the people, "Don't be afraid of them. Remember the Lord, who is great and

awesome, and fight for your brothers, your sons and your daughters, your wives and your homes."

When our enemies heard that we were aware of their plot and that God had frustrated it, we all returned to the wall, each to his own work.

Nehemiah 4:7-15 *NIV*

When the people started to get discouraged, Nehemiah told them not to give up. He knew that their God would fight for them. He also knew that God would strengthen them and enable them to finish their assigned task. So Nehemiah assigned half of the people to go up on the wall to work and the other half to stay down and guard the wall with weapons. In addition, those who did the work of construction had to carry a sword with them at all times (vv. 16-18).

The people obeyed Nehemiah's instructions and kept on working hard; meanwhile, God worked behind the scenes to confuse and confound the plans of the enemy. Finally, the people completed their task; Jerusalem had strong walls once more.

As you enter into your new season, you will have to adopt the same strategy Nehemiah did when he and the other Jews entered into their new season of rebuilding what had earlier been destroyed. You're going to have to make up your mind that you have a heart to *work* and that you will *stay on guard*. If you'll do that, God will be faithful to fight for you and to strengthen you for the task — and in the Name of Jesus, you *will* finish!

> ...Make up your mind that you have a heart to work and that you will stay on guard.

FINISHING THE RACE SET BEFORE US

It's so important that we not only work hard to fulfill an assignment God has given us, but that we also *finish* the task, no matter what it takes. This principle reminds me of a true Olympic story I once read regarding a Tanzanian marathon runner in the 1970s.

> Hours behind the runners in front of him, the last marathon runner finally entered the Olympic stadium. By that time, the drama of the day's events was almost over, and most of the spectators had gone home. This athlete's story, however, was still being played out. Limping into the arena, the Tanzanian runner grimaced with every step, his knees bleeding and bandaged from an earlier fall. His ragged appearance immediately caught the attention of the remaining crowd who cheered him on to the finish line. Why did he stay in the race? What made him endure his injuries to the end? When asked these questions later, he replied, "My country did not send me 7,000 miles away to start a race. They sent me 7,000 miles to *finish* the race."[19]

The thought of this Tanzanian runner's absolute determination to finish that natural race provokes something in me when I think of our spiritual race. We need that same gritty determination to finish the race God has set before each one of us! Jesus has paid too great a price for us to stay at the starting gate, stuck in the bondage from which He gave His life to free us!

Allowing bondage of any kind to remain in our lives will eat us up on the inside and hold us back in our old,

---

[19] Charles Swindoll, *Tale of the Tardy Oxcart* (Nashville: Word Publishing, 1998), p. 210.

stale seasons. As long as we stay in that place of bondage, we'll never see what God has for us up ahead.

But you don't have to stay in bondage. God will fight for you. He will strengthen you. You just have to declare it: "There is no turning around for me! I'm on the down ramp. I'm in a new season. It will take some work, and I'll have to stay on guard, but I'm going to finish the race God has set before me!"

So press, reach, and mark all progress. As you note and celebrate every new sign of progress, you will create momentum in your life — and that's exactly what you need to propel you to the next season. Momentum helps you do what you cannot do without it.

When I was growing up, there was a steep hill in front of our trailer park that I and my friends liked to ride up and down on our bikes. To make it all the way up the hill without stopping, we would sometimes back up into the carport of my home so we could have a level place to build up some speed before we started up the hill. That momentum made it a lot easier for us to ride all the way to the top than if we had started right at the bottom of that steep hill. And the best part was the reward for making it to the top — a fast coasting ride all the way back down the hill!

I can almost guarantee you that you have some hills to climb on the way to the next season, so make sure you've released every unnecessary weight from the past. Then strain and stretch forward with all your strength, marking all progress and celebrating your momentum. You've decided and declared that you're in a new season — so start acting like it, thinking like it, rejoicing like it, planning like it, talking like it, and smiling like it. It won't be long before you realize that you're actually enjoying the new season you first received by faith!

HOW TO CONDUCT YOURSELF IN THE NEW SEASON

6

*O*nce you get out of an undesirable situation and enter your new season, there is one thing you *don't* want to do — you don't want to make the same mess and land yourself right back in your old season! Furthermore, you don't want to live irresponsibly and create a *new* mess.

A lot of people do just that and, as a result, live their lives in recycled old seasons. God may deliver them out of a bad season and give them a fresh start. But instead of behaving wisely in their brand-new season, they create problems for themselves that could have been avoided and end up recycling their old mess!

You need to keep in mind that there is always another season after your present season. That means you can never live in a sloppy manner if you want the next season to be better than the one you're in now.

Remember, God has called you to go from glory to glory. He intends for your latter days to be greater than your former days. Your path is to shine ever brighter unto the perfect day.

That means your best days are still ahead! You should be continually moving on and going higher in the things of God, for His plan always involves preservation and increase. In other words, whatever blessings God brings into your life will not only be preserved but will increase — *if* you conduct yourself properly in your new season.

> You should be continually moving on and going higher in the things of God, for His plan always involves preservation and increase.

That's why it's so important that you know how to conduct yourself in this new season you have just entered. If you don't learn that lesson — if you neglect to seek God and end up wandering through this new season without divine direction — you won't make it very far. Before long you'll begin to behave unwisely. You won't make the needed preparations, or you'll fail to sow right, think right, or act right. Eventually you'll find yourself in a bigger mess than you were in before.

So how do you avoid making a new mess in your new season? First, you must realize that entering a new season doesn't mean everything will immediately be full grown and in place. Remember, this process of following God's plan from one season to the next is all about *transformation*, not about *self-improvement*. You have to experience real, genuine change on the inside.

You can't come into a new season and act like your same old, goofy self. You also can't just whitewash your faults and shortcomings and hope that God won't notice! If you are going to experience the future and the hope God has set out before you, you'll first have to be willing to make any adjustments, clarifications, and changes the Holy Spirit leads you to make.

We're going to look at several keys that will help you know how to properly conduct yourself in a new season. But be forewarned — it's going to take some diligent effort and commitment on your part, even when you don't feel like trying. You can't live your life depending on spiritual or emotional highs, always looking for something to feel blessed or excited about. This transformation process is a day-by-day, hammer-and-nail, chisel-and-saw process.

However, God promises to grace you and to help you in this process. Yes, you have to follow through on the principles He sets forth in His Word. But as you honor God's principles, He will honor your obedience by releasing His power into any situation you might encounter along the way.

I know you don't want to go back to that old season you just left behind. Furthermore, you want to receive and fully enjoy everything God desires for you to harvest in this new season and in all the seasons to come.

What is the nature of your future seasons? You can't know that right now, although you may harbor certain hopes about what those seasons might hold. However, you *can* make sure you are keeping things moving in the right direction and in divine order. As you are faithful to do that, God will be faithful to navigate you from one season to the next according to His timing and design.

FORGET AND PRESS

First, we need to continue to apply the principles that brought us into the new season in the first place. We must *decide, declare, release,* and *reach.*

We've already talked about these principles, but I want to take the discussion a little further. You see, the same principles that got you out of the old season will keep you moving forward through the new season to an ever-brighter future in God. With that in mind, let's look at Philippians 3:13,14 one more time:

> **Brethren, I do not count myself to have appre-hended; but one thing I do, forgetting those things which are behind and reaching forward to those things which are ahead,**
> **I press toward the goal for the prize of the upward call of God in Christ Jesus.**

The only way to distance yourself from the old season is to *release* and *reach.* You have to forget what lies behind and continue to press ahead. You may have walked through the doorway of your new season, but you have to keep on moving because there will eventually be another doorway to walk through. If you just hang out at the doorway, thinking about the place you left behind, you'll never find the next open door. You might even find yourself slipping backwards out the door you just entered!

Think back to what it used to be like on the last day of school before summer break. The moment that final bell rang, you were out of there! You wanted to go fish or play ball. You *didn't* want to sit around and think about your math class! Why did you want to forget about it? Because you were in a new season! You weren't going to enjoy yourself in that new season if you spent all your time thinking about that old season of doing homework and taking exams!

I recently received a phone call from a minister friend of mine who had been hospitalized with chest pain due to stress. I called him back to check on him. I knew he had been going through a rough time physically for quite a while.

When I finally got my friend on the telephone, he immediately started talking about the problem. Finally, I stopped him and said, "Listen, man, the very thing that slammed you into that hospital bed is what you won't quit talking about! You have to stop that. Talk about something else. You should be preaching tomorrow in your church. Instead, you will be lying in a hospital bed with a tube in your arm while they work on you and keep a watch on your condition. Stop thinking and talking about your problem!" (Now, I don't talk to everyone like this. This man had given me that place in his life, so I felt free to speak what was on my heart to him.)

I prayed for this minister and spoke peace to him. He thanked me for my prayer — but then he started talking about his problem again! I said to him, "I'm going to reach through this phone and put tape on your mouth if you don't stop talking about your problem!"

Remember, friend, your mind is your mind, and your mouth is your mouth. You can decide what you think and talk about. Why would you want to dwell on problems that belong back in your old seasons? Why would you want to talk about things that pull you down?

No, it's up to you to choose your thoughts and your words carefully. If you want to experience success in this new season, you have to *forget* the negative things that lie behind you in the past; then just keep pressing forward to those better, higher, *greater* things that God reserves for those who are diligent to obey!

WATCH YOUR WORDS

Second, you need to watch your words as you walk through your new season. Remember, your world is framed by the words of your mouth.

With that in mind, I want to give you an excellent verse to continually speak over your life. It's found in Romans 8:28:

And we know that all things work together for good to those who love God, to those who are the called according to His purpose.

I personalize that verse and say it this way: *"Everything always works out for me!"*

I remember something my mom used to say that contradicts that verse: "They say all good things must come to an end." I always wondered when I heard that, *Who is "they"? And why is it that the good things have to come to an end? How about all bad things coming to an end?*

Storms come, but storms go. They start, but they stop. God is telling us that we can perpetuate whatever we want to by the words of our mouths! It's time that we make a habit of speaking *good* things over our lives.

"I'm not a loser; I'm a winner. I'm not just a winner — I'm an *overcomer*. I can do all things through Christ who strengthens me!"

How are you going to do it?

"I don't know, but God will show me. I am led by the Holy Spirit, who gives me perfect knowledge of what to do in every situation!"

Declare good things over yourself, your marriage, your finances, your health, and your business. *Don't use your own mouth to speak against your future and your hope.*

If you have a goal in front of you, declare, "I'm heading toward that goal. I'm breathing down its neck. I am almost there. I'm pressing on. God will help me!"

If you have a need, start declaring, "God supplies all my needs according to His riches in glory by Christ Jesus. He will show me how to do these things. He will rebuke the devourer for my sake. My steps are ordered of the Lord. No weapon formed against me will prosper. Every tongue that rises up against me in judgment, I condemn it and declare that it will not bring me harm, for God watches over me and keeps me safe."

> *Don't use your own mouth to speak against your future and your hope.*

There are all sorts of good things you can say. Why would you put all that other junk in your mouth when you have the life-giving truth of God's Word to declare?

One of the best scriptures you can declare over yourself is Second Corinthians 5:21: "For God made Jesus who knew no sin to be sin for me, that I might become the right-eousness of God in Christ!"

You may find it difficult to call yourself righteous. But it was the blood of Jesus that made you righteous, not your own performance. If you believe that Jesus shed His blood for you and that His blood was enough to cleanse you of your sins, then you are the righteousness of God in Christ Jesus. You need to continually speak that truth over your life so your heart can grab hold of it!

Proverbs 12:6 says, *"...The mouth of the upright will deliver them."* God delivers us by our words. We therefore cooperate with His plans and purposes for our lives by con-tinually making sure that the words of our mouths line up with His Word.

Proverbs 6:2 shows the other side of this principle: *"You are snared by the words of your mouth; you are taken by the words of your mouth."* So it's possible to first be "snared" or caught in the trap and then "taken" or thrown in the pot to be cooked — all by the negative words of your mouth!

In other words, with the words of our mouths we can either be delivered or ensnared. Unfortunately, most of us are well familiar with the negative side of this principle. We don't know when to stop talking and therefore get our-selves in trouble.

One night when I was out riding with the local sheriff's department, I encountered a young man who definitely fit this description. We received a call about a disturbance at a convenience store. Three young men had gotten rude and obnoxious with the store clerk and caused some trouble before leaving.

When we caught the three young men, two of them were humble, apologetic, and cooperative. One of the sheriff's deputies talked to them a moment and then didn't have much else to do with them. But the other teenager wouldn't stop running his mouth! The deputies warned him. They told him that they were willing to go easy on him and just give him a warning but that he needed to watch his mouth. But the young man wouldn't listen. He just kept yelling crude, insolent remarks at the deputies, refusing to turn off that mouth of his.

Finally, one of the deputies told the rude teenager, "Out of the seven of us standing here, you're the only one not going home tonight!" Even that didn't stop this young man's foul mouth. To make a long story short, before the night was over, he was pepper-sprayed, hand-cuffed, put in a police car, and driven off to jail — ensnared, trapped, and thrown in a pot by the words of his own mouth!

Proverbs 14:3 says, *"In the mouth of a fool is a rod of pride, but the lips of the wise will preserve them."* The words of your mouth will not only deliver you — they will *preserve* you. Another translation says, *"...the lips of the wise will keep them safe."*[20] The *New English Bible* says, *"...a wise man's words are his safeguard."*[21]

Remember, we're talking about conducting ourselves properly in a new season. So much of it has to do with the words we speak. Proverbs 18:20,21 gives us more insight into the reason why:

---

[20] *The Bible in Basic English,* as quoted in *The Bible From 26 Translations,* p. 1194.
[21] *The New English Bible,* as quoted in *The Bible From 26 Translations,* p. 1194.

A man's stomach shall be satisfied from the fruit of his mouth; from the produce of his lips he shall be filled.

Death and life are in the power of the tongue, and those who love it will eat its fruit.

Just as your words were a key factor in leaving the old season and entering the new one, your words are now a key factor to your preservation and increase in your new season. Never allow your mouth to speak against your future and your hope. Never use your own mouth to speak against your goals, dreams, desires, and what you know God has for you. Instead, use your mouth for deliverance. Use your mouth for preservation. Use your mouth for life instead of destruction or death. *Be very careful not to set a trap for yourself with the words of your mouth!*

There are so many negative things you may have learned to say over the years. For instance, you may have a habit of saying, "I mess up all the time. God brings good things in my life, but I just have a way of making a mess of things. I can get a job, but I can't keep a job."

You need to stop saying that, and you need to start saying good things about yourself. The Bible says that you are to reign in life as a king (Rev. 5:10). As the king of your life, is that what you want to decree over your future? Or do you want your future seasons to be full of victory and success? If your answer is the latter, you need to start speaking positive, Word-based words about yourself!

Not only do you need to be careful about the kind of words you *speak*; you also need to be careful about the words you *hear*. That's exactly what Jesus said to His disciples in Mark 4:24:

Then He said to them, "Take heed what you hear. With the same measure you use, it will be measured to you; and to you who hear, more will be given."

Why is it important for us to be careful about what we hear? Because everything and everyone is talking. We live in the information age, and we get information from all directions. Cable television seems to offer innumerable channels. News shows and talk shows all talk about the same kinds of things. Even toys talk! But most all of it is noise pollution, and it's up to us to choose carefully which words we allow to impact *us. We* choose the words we hear; no one else does it for us.

And remember, it doesn't matter what anyone calls you; it just matters what you answer to! If you hear someone call you something you were in another season, don't receive that as your present identity. The only thing that matters is this: *Who are you becoming right now?*

> ...It's up to us to choose carefully which words we allow to impact us

The truth is, the words other people speak *to* you and *about* you can impact you greatly, so you need to be careful about what kind of words you allow yourself to hear. Don't let others' negative, critical words affect the way you perceive yourself. Whenever you're tempted to get discouraged by negative words spoken into your life, stand on God's promise in Isaiah 54:17:

"No weapon formed against you shall prosper, and every tongue which rises against you in judgment you shall condemn. This is the heritage of the servants of the Lord, and their righteousness is from Me," says the Lord.

On the other hand, you receive a very positive effect on your life when you hear words that are wise, godly, encouraging, faith-building, and challenging. Therefore, you should seek out people who will speak edifying words into your life.

I recently ran across a story that illustrates this point:

> One evening in New York, Steve Jobs of Apple Computers tried, as he had tried on several occasions, to recruit John Scully away from Pepsi-Cola to come run Apple Computers. No amount of money seemed enough to persuade Scully. Finally, in desperation, Steve Jobs said to Scully, "Do you want to spend the rest of your life making sugared water, or do you want to help us change the world?" It was as if he had been hit by a stiff punch to the stomach, Scully would later recall. This question of significance had bored its way into the interior of his life. It had to have gone to Scully's heart and flourished, because soon he was on his way westward to join up with Apple Computers.[22]

Sometimes the words people speak have such great significance that they change the hearer on the inside. For instance, when I played trumpet in my junior high band, our band director was a wonderful, wise man named Jesse Holliman. He was a trumpet player as well, and he worked with me a lot. I would go in to see him before school, during lunch, and after school so he could work with me and encourage me in my development as a trumpet player.

Mr. Holliman would always call a person "baby" when he was saying wise things to him or her. For instance, I'd finish my music theory test as quickly as I could and then run up to the front to turn it in because I wanted to be the

---

[22] Swindoll, op. cit.

first one done in the class. As I'd lay my finished test on Mr. Holliman's desk, he'd say, "Haste makes waste, Baby" — a comment that always made me ask if I could take my test back to my desk to check it one more time! Yes, Mr. Holliman was *full* of wisdom — truly a wonderful man.

Later during my high school years, our marching band was invited to play in a national parade. We started a fundraising drive to raise the thousands of dollars needed for us all to go. In the course of time, one set of parents realized that some of the band members going on this trip hadn't worked as hard as their dear son had to raise money. So the parents raised a fuss about the matter and started drawing other people into the argument.

The parents who started the dispute said, "We've worked hard, and these other people haven't worked hard at all — yet they're getting the same reward. That just isn't fair." The schism continued to escalate until I finally got drawn into the argument as well. I decided along with the rest of the disgruntled band players that we weren't going to go on the trip. Of course, that just meant we had signed up to be losers. We were the ones who had worked hard, yet now we were going to give it all away!

Then Mr. Holliman got wind of the situation and came over to my house. He parked at the end of my driveway and waited for someone to notice. My mom saw him and told me that he was there, so I went out and invited him in. Mr. Holliman declined, saying he just wanted to talk to me alone for a moment. Then he said, "I understand you're not going on this big trip."

I gave him my spiel, but I couldn't look him in the eye while I was doing it.

He said, "Yeah, I can see your point. But, Baby, just be able to say for yourself, 'I did my part.'"

Could I say I had done my part in the fundraising effort? Yes. Then why would I sign up with losers and grumblers?

I called my high school band director that night and apologized for refusing to go on the trip. Then I asked if I could still go on the trip. The band director said yes, and I had a wonderful time — all because of Mr. Holliman's words to me that day. But long after that particular experience was over, those words became woven into the fiber of my soul: No matter what endeavor I committed myself to in the future, *I just needed to be able to say that I had done my part.*

These are the kinds of words that can impact you on the inside and create a resolve in you that says, "If it's just me and Jesus, we'll get it done. It doesn't matter *what* anyone else does!" In every situation of life, there will be someone who isn't pulling his weight, who doesn't follow through and then makes excuses. But you will live your life a whole lot happier if you will decide on the inside, *I did MY part.*

A couple of years ago when I was going through a rough situation, a dear woman of God named Lynne Hammond spoke to me at a meeting we were both attending. She said, "Tim, do you know the plan of God? Find the plan of God and pursue it." This was another instance when powerful words became woven deep on the inside of me, helping me determine the right way to go both in that specific situation and in all the future challenges yet to come.

When you hear life-giving words that impact you like those words impacted me, *hold on* to them for all you're worth. On the other hand, when negative words become woven to the inside of your soul, you need to use the power in God's Word to tear them out. Those kinds of words hinder and limit your life and keep you stuck in undesirable seasons.

It's up to you. You determine what words you're going to allow to impact you. So make the decision to listen only to the words of the wise and godly. Let those words sink deep into your heart and impact your life for the better as you move with God through your new season.

Do Your Words Release or Bind?

Our words are either going to *release* us, or they're going to *bind* us. I once watched a secular talk show in which a doctor made a comment along this line, saying that our thoughts and our words have an immediate impact on our bodies and an eventual impact on our circumstances. That doctor was talking from a natural perspective, but his words were scriptural nonetheless.

It all goes back to this principle: *Your attitude determines success or failure.* I'm talking not only about your general frame of mind, but about the way you approach difficult situations. Your words and your thoughts have an *immediate* impact on your body, and they have an *eventual* impact on the circumstances that surround you. Your words will either release you, or your words will bind you.

That's why it's so important to build your life on the Word of God. What has God said over you? The answer lies in the Word. You need to start declaring, "This is my Bible. I am what it says I am. I have what it says I have. I can do what it says I can do!"

> Your words will either release you, or your words will bind you.

What has Jesus spoken about you? According to His perspective, who are you? What do you have? What can you do? You need to know these things from God's Word so you can release God's power in your life as you build a rock-solid foundation of faith.

In Luke 24:32, the two disciples asked each other, *"...Did not our heart burn within us while He* [Jesus] *talked with us on the road, and while He opened the Scriptures to us?"* That kind of reaction was common when Jesus taught the Word. Many times people were astonished by Jesus' teachings because He spoke words of life they had never heard before.

Those same words of life are now available to you whenever you want to read them, meditate on them, or hear them preached! So feed on the Word continually. Let those life-giving words sink deep down on the inside of you. The words of God are sharper than any two-edged sword, well able to release you from every stronghold that has bound you and hindered your progress in the past.

PROMISED LAND OR WILDERNESS? IT'S ALL IN OUR WORDS

There are two key categories of words with which you need to fill your mouth and your life: 1) words that recall what God *has done* for you, and 2) words that declare what God *will do* for you.

We can find this principle demonstrated in the account of the twelve Israelite spies in Numbers 13. When the Israelites finally reached the border of Canaan, Moses sent in spies to spy out the land. Those spies came back with the report that the land was good and spacious, with enough room for all its inhabitants to do what they had in their hearts. Instead of being a cramped, tight, pressure-filled, stressful place, it was wide open and free.

The spies also reported that it was a rich land that flowed with milk and honey. I did a little research to find out what that phrase "flowing with milk and honey" meant. This was an agricultural nation. Its people made their living and sustained themselves by their livestock and their produce. The land was so good and so rich that the people's cattle and goats grew up remarkably healthy and multiplied abundantly, producing so much milk that it was as if the land was *flowing* with milk. In the same way, the fruits and vegetables produced from the land were so sweet that it was as if the land was flowing with honey.

Just how rich was this land? Numbers 13:23 gives us a better clue:

> **Then they came to the Valley of Eshcol, and there cut down a branch with one cluster of grapes; they carried it between two of them on a pole. They also brought some of the pomegranates and figs.**

Now, what I'm about to say sounds incredible, but I was able to obtain commentaries of some of the ancient rabbis so I could get their take on the original Hebrew language. These rabbis say the language used here literally means that when the spies came back with figs and pomegranates to show the people, the fruit was so large that it took one man to carry one fig or one pomegranate! And when they cut one cluster of grapes to take back with them, it had to be hung on a double pole and carried by a number of men!

But even though the spies heaped praise on the merit of the land God had promised them, ten of them still brought back an evil report of doubt and unbelief. They told the people, "Truly, this land does flow with milk and honey, but we can't take it. The challenge is too big for us, for there are giants in the land." These spies messed up when they got on the wrong side of the "but"!

Joshua and Caleb were the only two spies who spoke the right kind of words about the Promised Land. After the other ten spies had stirred up the people with their bad report, Caleb stilled the crowd and told them to be quiet. Then he said, "Let's go up into the land, for we are well able to take it!" (v. 30).

The other ten spies said, "No, we can't. We're grasshoppers in their sight!" Why did they say that? Because they were grasshoppers in their own sight as well!

Of those twelve spies, only Joshua and Caleb eventually entered the Promised Land — the two who said, "We are able to take the land." What was the difference that allowed those two to enter in and the other ten spies to die in the wilderness? The only difference I could find was in *the words of their mouths*.

The same thing is true of the rest of that unbelieving generation of Israelites. They listened to the wrong kind of words and started speaking those words of doubt and unbelief out of their own mouths. As a result, all those millions remained in the wilderness until they died, never entering in to the land God had promised them.

Your words either release you, or your words bind you. Therefore, if you want to enter that spacious, open place that God has prepared for you, you will have to line up the words in your mouth and the thoughts in your mind with the Word of God. You'll have to start speaking with the spirit of faith, saying such things as, "I am well able to do this! God brings me out that He might bring me into a good land, a spacious land, a land that flows with milk and honey."

Remember, we're not talking about Heaven here; we're talking about the here and now. If you want to enjoy the fullness of God's plan for you in this new season, you need to fill your mouth with words that recall what He *has already done* for you and declare what He *will do* for you. As you are faithful to speak the right kind of words, God will be faithful to show you the length, breadth, and width of your personal promised land!

WATCH YOUR STEP

The third key to properly conducting yourself in a new season is to *watch your step*. This principle can be found in Psalm 37:23:

> **The steps of a good man are ordered by the Lord, and He delights in his way.**

The word "ordered" in this verse literally means in the Hebrew *to set up*.[23] This means God has set up a particular

---

[23] Strong, "The Hebrew Dictionary of the Old Testament," #3559.

path in front of you — a path that requires certain steps to be taken in order for you to stay on course. However, this requirement isn't a difficult one to fulfill because you have God's wonderful promise in Proverbs 3:5,6 to claim:

> **Trust in the Lord with all your heart, and lean not on your own understanding;**
> **In all your ways acknowledge Him, and He shall direct your paths.**

God will direct you in the path He has set up for you to follow. Remember, Isaiah 40:4 says that God will make your high places low and your low places level. He will make your crooked places straight, and He will make your rough places smooth.

We love it whenever God intervenes to supernaturally improve the situations we face. But God also has a remedy for those times when He *doesn't* immediately change our difficult situation. If God doesn't pave our road, He will give us off-road equipment to navigate around the obstacles!

That's what Psalm 18:33 (*KJV*) is talking about when it says, *"He maketh my feet like hinds' feet, and setteth me upon my high places."* In other words, you will have sure-footed stability even on the rocks, crags, and cliffs of life. You'll be able to outrun your enemy in any terrain. Either way you will come out the victor in every situation — as long as you stay alert and watch your step.

According to Romans 8:14, the Holy Spirit is endeavoring to lead you in every aspect of your life: *"For as many as are led by the Spirit of God, these are sons of God."* But you have to pay attention and get quiet in your heart in order to discern what step you should take next, for the Holy Spirit's leading seldom comes in spectacular or obvious ways.

Sometimes when a road is being built, the construction crews will put up orange cones, concrete barricades, or sawhorses with blinking lights to steer drivers away from the construction zone. But when you drive through that part of the road, you'll invariably find cones knocked over, someone's fender lying next to the concrete, and tire skid marks everywhere. Why? Because some drivers just weren't paying attention!

Proverbs 4:10-12 tells you some of the benefits of paying attention to the Holy Spirit's "orange cones" as He endeavors to direct your path and order your steps:

> **Hear, my son, and receive my sayings, and the years of your life will be many.**
> **I have taught you in the way of wisdom; I have led you in right paths.**
> **When you walk, your steps will not be hindered, and when you run, you will not stumble.**

We looked at Ephesians 5:15 earlier, which says, *"See then that you walk circumspectly, not as fools but as wise."* We saw that the word "circumspectly" denotes *circular* or *from all sides*. However, "circumspectly" also means *carefully*. You have to walk carefully through life, taking your time as you look for that next step you need to take. And where do you look? In the Word of God, for it is a lamp unto your feet and a light unto your path to make that path easy to see.

> ...Walk carefully through life, taking your time as you look for that next step you need to take.

211

No matter what you are facing, by the authority of God's Word there is a next step for you. You need to seek God to find out what that next step is. You don't want to miss it, because that might mean you miss all the subsequent steps that come after the one you're supposed to take next!

You may say, "But I just don't know what to do. I feel like I'm up against the wall." That may well be true, but God is going to show you how to move that wall, how to go through that wall, or how to turn around and get back on the right path if you've taken a wrong turn. You don't have to try to figure it out yourself. All you have to do is let Him show you the next step to take.

I hate to miss an exit when I'm driving. When I have to travel to a big city, I like to get a GPS unit in my rental cars because it tells me how to get to my destination and where to turn. However, sometimes that directional unit can't tell me what I need to know, and I either miss my turn or make a wrong one. I don't like the feeling I get in that situation when I read a sign that says, "Next Exit 407 Miles"!

In life, we've all "missed our exit" at one time or another. But God always provides a way back to the right path. He will help us no matter how far we've gotten off track. We just need to trust Him as we walk carefully before Him and look to Him to show us our next step.

Here's a thought you may not have considered: Your next step may be the one right behind you. You may need to turn around! Let me give you two scriptures that tell you why this could be necessary:

> **Do not enter the path of the wicked, and do not walk in the way of evil.**

Avoid it, do not travel on it; turn away from it and pass on.

Proverbs 4:14,15

Remove your way far from her [the immoral woman], **and do not go near the door of her house.**

Proverbs 5:8

These are just a few of the scriptures that point to this principle: *The long way is better than the wrong way.* Typically, the things that pulled on us before we came to the Lord still pull on us. Yes, we're born again and we are renewing our minds, but our flesh still likes the things it always liked.

Just because you've been on good behavior for three months, don't tell your flesh it can have a "flesh day" to celebrate. If you do, you'll get in trouble. You'll probably get pepper-sprayed! You just can't trust your flesh. You have to continually keep your body under and keep your thoughts guarded by the Word. This is all part of watching your step, because *whatever you give your attention to is the thing you'll be drawn to.*

There are all kinds of things that can pull on you in life — from obviously negative things such as whiskey, drugs, and pornography to seemingly innocent things like chocolate or food. If you're like many folks, you may have a refrigerator pulling on you! You may be sitting in the living room when all of a sudden you hear it calling from the kitchen, "Come on in here and check me out, big boy!"

The television can also talk to you, pulling on you to the point of distraction at times. If that is the case — if your television set is creating problems in your walk with God — you would do well to get rid of it. Remember, the long way is better than the wrong way.

Or perhaps you have to pass by the ABC Liquor Store on the way to church. If alcohol had a pull on your life in times past and it still pulls on you while you're waiting at the stoplight, don't look around to see if anyone from the church can see you slip over to buy a bottle. And don't go looking for a new church either. You just need to find a new way to church! Or maybe you need to call three buddies and give them a ride to church with you. Do whatever it takes to stay on the right path, for the long way is better than the wrong way!

Another important part of watching your step is to *make sure you keep your balance*, for all extremes lead to error. Perhaps someone laid hands on you and prophesied over you in the past. If that experience helped you in your spiritual walk, receive it thankfully, because God certainly does works through other people in that way. However, don't conclude that this is now the only way you can receive from God. Or if you received revelation from God as you were praying, don't think that you don't need church anymore and that you only need to pray. Prayer is very important to your spiritual life, but you still need balance.

You need *all* that God has provided for you: the Word, prayer, manifestations of the Spirit, church, and godly people who will encourage you in the things of God. You also have to live in the real world that operates according to certain natural laws. For instance, you can't believe God for healing in the Sunday morning church service and then go home and eat like a garbage truck! That's why staying balanced is one of the most important keys to watching your step and successfully moving through the seasons of life.

OBEY GOD

If you are going to make it through your new season without making a new mess, you are going to have to obey God without question, for He is the only One who knows the path set out for you. Obedience doesn't require explanation. When God says it, you are to do it, trusting that He knows more than you know.

> When God says it, you are to do it, trusting that He knows more than you know.

However, I'm not just talking about obedience alone. God desires obedience with a right heart and a right attitude. We can see this in the following scriptures:

> "Oh, that they had such a heart in them that they would fear Me and always keep all My commandments, that it might be well with them and with their children forever!"
>
> **Deuteronomy 5:29**

> "If you are willing and obedient, you will eat the best from the land;
>   but if you resist and rebel, you will be devoured by the sword." For the mouth of the Lord has spoken.
>
> **Isaiah 1:19,20**

You have to have the right attitude — to be not only obedient but *willing,* obeying God from your heart. The only way to truly hear and receive from God is to do His will from a sincere heart of love.

Psalm 112:1 gives us more insight into the attitude God desires to see in us:

Blessed is the man who fears the Lord, who **DELIGHTS GREATLY** in His commandments.

My paraphrase for this verse is this: "I *love* God telling me what to do!"

Think about it. God has been so gracious, kind, and merciful to us that He brought us out of our messes so He could bring us into new seasons of blessing and peace. How could we assume even for a moment that we might not have to listen to Him? We'd be foolish to think that we can leave an old season and then decide not to obey God.

No, God brings His people out so they can obey Him and fulfill His purposes on this earth. Psalm 105 tells us this was true with the children of Israel, and it is still true today.

He also brought them out with silver and gold, and there was none feeble among His tribes.
Egypt was glad when they departed, for the fear of them had fallen upon them.
He spread a cloud for a covering, and fire to give light in the night.
The people asked, and He brought quail, and satisfied them with the bread of heaven.
He opened the rock, and water gushed out; it ran in the dry places like a river.
For He remembered His holy promise, and Abraham His servant.
He brought out His people with joy, His chosen ones with gladness.
He gave them the lands of the Gentiles, and they inherited the labor of the nations,
That they might observe His statutes and keep His laws. Praise the Lord!

Psalm 105:37-45

I like the way the *Amplified* version says it in verse 45:

That they might observe His statutes and keep His laws [hearing, receiving, loving, and obeying them]. Praise the Lord! (Hallelujah!)

God brings you out so that He might bring you in, always for your good and always to preserve you. God has good things in mind for you. If He tells you to do something, you can trust that it is for your own good. Don't try to outsmart, out-think, second-guess, or negotiate with God. If God says to do something, then do it. And don't just do it — *love* to do it!

> God brings you out so that He might bring you in, always for your good and always to preserve you.

BE THANKFUL

God brought you out of that tight, cramped old season so He could bring you into a broad and open place of abundant living. Once you are in your new season, it is very important that you show your thankfulness to the Lord for His goodness and mercy to you.

Psalm 107 reveals this scriptural pattern for deliverance. First, we cry out to God; second, He hears our prayers and delivers us from our bondage and distress; and third, we give thanks to Him, "declaring His works with rejoicing":

Then they cried out to the Lord in their trouble, and He saved them out of their distresses.
He brought them out of darkness and the shadow of death, and broke their chains in pieces.

Oh, that men would give thanks to the Lord for His goodness, and for His wonderful works to the children of men!

For He has broken the gates of bronze, and cut the bars of iron in two.

Fools, because of their transgression, and because of their iniquities, were afflicted.

Their soul abhorred all manner of food, and they drew near to the gates of death.

Then they cried out to the Lord in their trouble, and He saved them out of their distresses.

He sent His word and healed them, and delivered them from their destructions.

Oh, that men would give thanks to the Lord for His goodness, and for His wonderful works to the children of men!

Let them sacrifice the sacrifices of thanksgiving, and declare His works with rejoicing.

Psalm 107:13-22

In Luke 17, we read the account of ten lepers who followed the first two steps of this divine pattern when they encountered Jesus and cried out to Him for their healing and deliverance. However, only one of those ten lepers remembered that all-important third step.

And it came to pass, as he went to Jerusalem, that he passed through the midst of Samaria and Galilee.

And as he entered into a certain village, there met him ten men that were lepers, which stood afar off:

And they lifted up their voices, and said, Jesus, Master, have mercy on us.

And when he saw them, he said unto them, Go shew yourselves unto the priests. And it came to pass, that, as they went, they were cleansed.

And one of them, when he saw that he was healed, turned back, and with a loud voice glorified God,

And fell down on his face at his feet, giving him thanks: and he was a Samaritan.

And Jesus answering said, Were there not ten cleansed? but where are the nine?

There are not found that returned to give glory to God, save this stranger.

And he said unto him, Arise, go thy way: thy faith hath made thee whole.

Luke 17:11-19 *KJV*

First, the ten lepers cried out to Jesus for help; then Jesus delivered them from their disease. It is the same pattern we saw in Psalm 107. When we cry out to God, He hears and delivers us. That's just the way our God is!

Jesus instructed the ten lepers to go to the priest. Under Levitical law, a leper who had been healed of his disease had to go before the priest so his healing could be verified. So the lepers chose to walk by faith and not by sight, obeying Jesus' instructions even though they didn't look or feel any different. And as a result of the ten lepers' obedience, they were all cleansed *as they went* (v. 14).

However, we see in verse 15 that only one of the ten went on to complete God's pattern of deliverance — and he wasn't even a Jew! When this one man saw that he was healed, he returned to Jesus and with a loud voice glorified God, falling down on his face at Jesus' feet to give thanks.

Jesus' questions to this one man reveals the importance He places on a thankful heart: "...*Were there not ten cleansed? But where are the nine? Were there not any found who returned to give glory to God except this foreigner?*" (vv. 17,18).

Jesus could count; He knew ten lepers had been cleansed on their way to see the priest. But Jesus was making a point. He wanted to know why only one of the ten returned to give thanks for what God had done for him when all ten lepers received the same cleansing from their disease.

Then Jesus turned to the man who had shown his gratitude and told him, *"...Arise, go thy way: thy faith hath made thee whole"* (v. 19). That word "whole," from the Greek word *sozo*, is something different than just being cleansed — something much better!

Let me suggest something to you that is implied by this word *sozo*. All ten obeyed Jesus' instructions to go to the priest, and all ten were cleansed of leprosy. In other words, they no longer had the disease in their lives. But the man who returned and gave thanks at the feet of Jesus was made *whole*.

Leprosy will eat away at a person's extremities — fingers, nose, and toes — until he actually loses those parts of his body. So when Jesus said to the one man who returned, "Your faith has made you whole," it's possible that the parts of that man's body destroyed by leprosy were restored to normal at that very moment. I can't prove it, but the power of the language suggests that this is what happened.

Now, let me ask you a question. When the leper abandoned what he was doing and returned to thank God for what He had done for him, did that stop his progress? No, it actually propelled this man ahead and *multiplied* his progress! He left Jesus' presence that day not only cleansed, but made whole from the disease that had laid waste to his body!

Whatever that word "whole" means here, the point is this: Something greater happened for the one man who gave thanks. In the same way, something gets multiplied in *your* life if you will return and give thanks to the One who blessed you.

That is the key: *Whenever you see something that God has done for you, return and give thanks.* When you are protected in traffic, thank God for it. When you get a good deal or when you get bumped up to first class on your airplane flight, recognize that God is moving on your behalf to give you favor. Whenever you see God's hand at work in your life, don't ignore it — return and give thanks.

We increase our capacity to receive when we thank God for what He does. This principle is found throughout the Word of God. Everything is small before it is big. You must be faithful in little before you can be faithful with much. So if you're not grateful for the smaller ways God is working in your life right now, why would He do something big in your life?

One of the main reasons many Christians are in poor spiritual health is that they don't have thankful hearts. God is at work in their lives in all kinds of ways, but they fail to ever notice it or thank Him for it.

> We increase our capacity to receive when we thank God for what He does.

Romans 1:21 tells us the danger of this kind of ingratitude toward the Lord: *"...Although they knew God, they did not glorify Him as God, nor were thankful, but became futile in their thoughts, and their foolish hearts were darkened."* The Greek reveals that these people got off the right path. So what is the way to stay on the right path? Thank God for every good thing He does for you. Actively look for what He has done. If you can only see two good things and forty-one bad things, look for those two things and thank God for them!

Staying on the right path in our new season is a very important consideration, for there will always be other doorways to go through. We certainly don't want to be stuck in the corner of the basement when it's time to enter the next season God has for us! His plan is to take us from *glory to glory*, not from *gory to gory*! God wants us to continually move forward toward the fullness of His plan for our lives, but to do that, we have to stay on the right path by being thankful to Him for blessing us in both big and small ways.

Hebrews 13:15 tells us how to show our thankfulness to God: *"Therefore by Him let us continually offer the sacrifice of praise to God, that is, the fruit of our lips, giving thanks to His name."* That phrase "the fruit of our lips" means that we are to *speak* our thankfulness to God, not just *think* it.

Psalm 92:1,2 also tells us that giving thanks and praise to God is something we do with the words of our mouths:

> **It is good to give thanks to the Lord, and to sing praises to Your name, O Most High;**
> **To declare Your lovingkindness in the morning,**
> **And Your faithfulness every night.**

You are to make mention that God's name is exalted and declare what He has done for you. That doesn't mean you have to go around declaring your thankfulness toward God to everyone you meet. Your declaration may be just between you and God, or you may have the opportunity to tell a few other people of like precious faith what He did for you. But the important point here is to *always remember to give thanks to God.*

Staying thankful helps you avoid becoming prideful. It keeps you aware of God's power and faithfulness and causes you to look at the true Source of help behind all you have accomplished in life.

If you just came out of a bad season, don't ever think it was your own skill and effort that brought you out. God is the One who delivered you, and He will continue to help you in your new season as you trust Him and continually thank Him for His goodness in your life.

Tell the Good News

God has just brought you out of a difficult season in victory; that means you have something to say. Therefore, an important part of conducting yourself properly in a new season is to *look for the right time to tell the good news.*

Certainly God didn't bring you out of a bad season so you could stand around with a goofy grin on your face! No, He brought you out so He could *use* you! He has brought you into a new season with new revelation and a new anointing. Now He wants you to get excited about what He has done in your life and *tell the good news!*

How can you know that this is what God desires of you? Just look at what the angel of the Lord said to the apostles in Acts 5:

> **Then the high priest rose up, and all those who were with him (which is the sect of the Sadducees), and they were filled with indignation,**
> **and laid their hands on the apostles and put them in the common prison.**

But at night an angel of the Lord opened the prison doors and brought them out, and said,

"Go, stand in the temple and speak to the people all the words of this life."

And when they heard that, they entered the temple early in the morning and taught....

Acts 5:17-21

Some of the apostles were ministering to people in the Name of Jesus, preaching the Word and healing the sick. God was performing miracles, signs, and wonders through the apostles. This upset the religious leaders so much that they threw the apostles in prison.

While the apostles sat in prison, however, an angel of the Lord came and supernaturally brought them out of that bad situation. Then the angel gave the apostles specific directions, telling them to *"Go, stand in the temple and speak to the people all the words of this life"* (v. 20).

As I meditated on this scripture, the word "temple" stood out to me. I believe it's significant that the angel of the Lord commanded the apostles to go to a specific location — the temple, which was a holy place.

A spiritual principle can be seen in the angel's instructions. There is a holy place and time to speak words of life into someone, and the Holy Spirit knows where and when that time and place is. Look for those divinely placed opportunities when God provides an entrance into the life of a coworker, a neighbor, a friend; then share with that person what God has done for you.

An old school of thought said that because we were called to preach the Gospel to the ends of the earth, we were to spray down everyone we met with our message.

But in this day we live in, God isn't asking us to preach to everyone who comes near us. Not everyone is ready to receive what we have to say. God wants us to be led by His Spirit, who knows exactly what's going on in the hearts of men.

So if God has brought you out of a season of heartache, failure, or loss into a new season of hope and blessing, look for a specific holy time and place to minister the good news to others. What good news? That God wants to bring them out of *their* bad season as well!

You might say something like this: "I understand you're going through a rough time. I went through some rough times myself in times past, but do you know what I did? I called on God, and He heard me and brought me out of that mess! God isn't a respecter of persons; if you'll call on Him, He'll help you too."

What did you just do by saying those words? You brought God into that person's situation!

If someone you know is going through a tough time right now and you've already come through a difficult season in victory, then you have something to say to that person. You are qualified to speak, so stay sensitive to the Holy Spirit and look for His specific holy place and time.

Ask that person if you can say something to him. Then without going into all the gory details, tell him how God brought you through that trial by His power and His grace. And if you sense the Holy Spirit saying that it isn't for you to tell that person the good news, just pray for him. God will honor your prayers by sending someone else to speak to him at His appointed time and place.

Hold Your Head Up High

You're in a new season now, so you need to carry yourself differently. After all, the land of promise is a lot different than the land of bondage from whence you came! If you were a slave to something in the old season and you're free now, you need to hold your head up high and smile like the free person you are!

That's exactly what God told His people in Leviticus 26:13 (*NIV*):

> **I am the Lord your God, who brought you out of Egypt so that you would no longer be slaves to the Egyptians; I broke the bars of your yoke and enabled you to walk with heads held high.**

I also like the way *The Living Bible* puts it:

> **For I am the Lord your God who brought you out of the land of Egypt, so that you would be slaves no longer; I have broken your chains and will make you walk with dignity.**

You have to realize deep down on the inside that you are no longer *where* you once were, and you are no longer *who* you once were. As Psalm 103:4 (*AMP*) says, you have a God *"Who redeems your life from the pit and corruption, Who beautifies, dignifies, and crowns you with loving-kindness and tender mercy."*

You need to declare over yourself that you are in a new season. You are free, forgiven, blessed, helped, and surrounded by favor. You are no longer in bondage to whatever held you back in times past. Therefore, you can hold your head up high and be confident!

One of the problems with the children of Israel was that even though God brought them out of slavery, slavery was still *in* them. As the old saying goes, "You can take the boy out of the country, but you can't take the country out of the boy!"

Don't let yourself be hindered by this same problem. You are in a new season and called to increase, so act like it. Think like it. Talk like it. Walk like it. Make plans like it.

You are also free from the sins and failures of the past, so carry yourself like that is true, both on the inside and the outside. You see, your body language says a lot. People can tell if you're feeling guilty, ashamed, depressed, and angry, or happy and free. But don't "strut your stuff" in a prideful way; just hold up your head and walk with dignity. It's perfectly all right to feel confident; after all, you're enjoying a new season because you have the favor of Almighty God!

> You are in a new season and called to increase, so act like it. Think like it. Talk like it.

Be Quick To Recover

Just because you're in a wonderful new season, don't assume that you won't have any more problems; that the devil won't bother you anymore; or that everything will go your way from now on. If you've been thinking along those lines, take heed! The moment you think you're standing, the enemy will come up on your blind side and clobber you!

I don't believe God for problems. I don't wake up in the morning and ask Him to give me something to overcome. I also don't taunt the devil to try his best shot at me. I believe

God will order my steps and surround me with favor. Meanwhile, I'll be careful and hold my head up high. I'll walk through this life believing for good, healthy, and prosperous days in my future.

Nevertheless, we can't get away from the fact that we have an enemy on this earth who roams about, seeking those of us he may devour (1 Peter 5:8). This enemy continually tries to trip us up. He isn't content to wave goodbye to us and then freely let us go without a fight.

You never have to live in fear of the devil. As long as you're not ignorant of his devices, he cannot take advantage of you. However, you have to realize that it isn't over between you and the enemy. The only way the devil is ever going to stop bothering you is for you to go home to be with the Lord!

Even when Jesus dealt with the enemy, the most He accomplished was to temporarily run him off with the sword of the Word as He declared, *"Devil, it is written..."* (Luke 4:4,8,12). Every time the devil left Jesus, it was only "for a season" (Luke 4:13 *KJV*). The Greek actually means *for a more opportune and susceptible time.*

Just because you run a varmint off your property doesn't mean it isn't coming back. Just because you scared the raccoon away from your garbage doesn't mean you won't have to do it again later on.

In the same way, the enemy will always look for a way to attack you again from another direction or with another strategy. And if he ever succeeds in knocking you down, should you lie in the mud and wallow? *No, you need to get up and have a quick recovery.*

We should have learned something by now from all those "Rocky" movies we've watched. For instance, if we get knocked down, we are to *get up* again — quickly, and with an attitude! We certainly better not whimper! And if all kinds of negative things get piled up on us while we're still down, we can at least run our mouths at our opponent. Then when we do get up, the devil better *know* that we're up again because of our powerful "one-two" punch of faith that knocks *him* down to the ground!

Psalm 37:23,24 has something important to say about this principle:

> **The steps of a good man are ordered by the Lord, and He delights in his way.**
> **Though he fall, he shall not be utterly cast down; for the Lord upholds him with His hand.**

The *Amplified Bible* says in verse 23 that the Lord *"...busies Himself with his every step."* The Lord busies Himself with the good man's every step, yet it's still possible for the good man to fall.

You don't plan on falling, and you don't try to fall — but you have an enemy who doesn't play fair and who loves to rain on your parade. What are you going to do when he does? Well, if your big balloon gets away, pull off your sock and make a sock puppet, and have a parade anyway! Remember, you're the righteousness of God in Christ, and the Bible says that although a righteous man may fall, he *always* gets up.

> **For though a righteous man falls seven times, he rises again, but the wicked are brought down by calamity.**
>
> **Proverbs 24:16 *NIV***

No matter how many times you trip them up, God-loyal people don't stay down long.

Proverbs 24:16 *Message*

Do not rejoice over me, my enemy; when I fall, I will arise; when I sit in darkness, the Lord will be a light to me.

Micah 7:8

So if the enemy succeeds in knocking you down during this new season, don't just lie there on the ground and talk against your future. Put all your effort into getting back up, and be very careful about what you say. Remember, you're in God's capable hands, and He will help you have a quick recovery.

The truth is, *spiritual maturity is measured by recovery time*. How long does it take you to get over a setback? In order to decrease the time it takes, you need to develop a deep resolve you can draw on as you stay connected to all the resources of Heaven.

> ...*Spiritual maturity is measured by recovery time. How long does it take you to get over a setback?*

You don't want any problems, but when problems trip you up and you find yourself face down in the gravel, what are you going to do? Lay hold of the divine resources at your disposal, and *get back up*! You might get knocked down, but you're not knocked out. And if you do get knocked down, you're not down for long. Why? Because you're in a new season, and you're not missing one beat of it!

Keep Short Accounts

Forgiveness is the real point of this particular key for conducting ourselves properly in a new season. We need to walk in forgiveness, and we need to receive forgiveness.

The Bible says we *all* sin and come short of the glory of God (Rom. 3:23). Yes, we are born again; yes, we are children of God. But we are still in our fleshy bodies, living in a world full of pressures and influences. Our minds are not fully renewed. Even though we don't want to sin — even though we don't plan on sinning — sometimes it still happens, and we usually have something to do with it.

We are redeemed from the penalty of sin; however, the effect of sin still exists in our lives. If left unchecked, sin bears down on us and weighs us down, keeping us from progressing in our walk with God. This is in part what the Bible is talking about when it says the wages of sin is death (Rom. 6:23). That's why it's so important that we keep ourselves continually cleansed of sin by the blood of Jesus.

If we don't have the confidence and joy that we know we should have as believers, we may try to blame it on a lot of other things. But more than likely, the root of our problem is that we haven't kept a short account with God. In other words, we may have unconfessed sin in our lives.

We may try to justify holding on to our unconfessed sin, saying things like, "I know I have a bad attitude, but let me tell you why..." But there's never an excuse for holding on to a bad attitude. We just need to be cleansed and forgiven of all our bad attitudes, no matter *why* we have them!

When I was a child, before my parents got a divorce, we lived first in a house and then in a trailer by a sewage treatment center. It didn't bother me too much to live that close to the treatment center. I would even walk out on the little bridge that extended over the circular tank to fly my kite. The treatment center was part of my world and the world was mine — although even as a kid, I had to admit that it *was* rather smelly!

The house we lived in had "terazzo" floors and no carpet. It seemed to me that my mom was always waxing those floors. I noticed, however, that before she could wax the floors, she first had to strip off the old wax. Otherwise, Mom told me, she'd only be waxing over a yellowish buildup of wax that would make our floors look ugly.

That's what sin is like when we don't avail ourselves to the cleansing power of the blood of Jesus. We develop a "waxy yellow sin buildup" — with unconfessed sin upon unconfessed sin — that must be stripped away before we can move on with God.

It is a wonderful thing to be forgiven, cleansed, refreshed, revived, renewed, and to have your joy restored. But in order to experience this in your own life, you have to keep a short account with God. As soon as you realize that something is wrong in your life, you need to respond to the tug of the Holy Spirit and get cleansed.

> **But if we walk in the light as He is in the light, we have fellowship with one another, and the blood of Jesus Christ His Son cleanses us from all sin.**
> **If we say that we have no sin, we deceive ourselves, and the truth is not in us.**

> If we confess our sins, He is faithful and just to forgive us our sins and to cleanse us from all unrighteousness.
>
> If we say that we have not sinned, we make Him a liar, and His word is not in us.
>
> My little children, these things I write to you, so that you may not sin. And if anyone sins, we have an Advocate with the Father, Jesus Christ the righteous.
>
> And He Himself is the propitiation for our sins, and not for ours only but also for the whole world.
>
> **1 John 1:7-2:2**

I am so thankful that First John 1:9 is in the Bible! If we sin, we are to confess our sins to the One whose very nature is faithful and just. When we say what God says about our behavior and we judge that sin out of our lives, then God is true to His own faithful nature to forgive us of our sins and to cleanse us from all unrighteousness.

This confession of your sin to God needs to happen on a regular basis. You shouldn't have one day every two months marked on your calendar so you can check for any sins you might need to take care of. You need to keep *short* accounts with God. As soon as you sense on the inside that you did something wrong, get things right with Him. Receive a fresh cleansing of the blood. Allow Him to restore your joy. Get revived, refreshed, and renewed all over again!

Not only must you receive forgiveness, you must also forgive others. If you are going to conduct yourself properly in a new season, you simply have to forgive.

Mark 11:25 (*AMP*) makes this point abundantly clear:

> And whenever you stand praying, if you have anything against anyone, forgive him and let it drop (leave

it, let it go), in order that your Father Who is in heaven may also forgive you your [own] failings and shortcomings and let them drop.

Notice the phrase, *"...if you have anything against anyone...."* That covers about everything, doesn't it? If we have anything against anyone, we need to forgive. The reason we often *don't* forgive is that we don't think God is going to deal with the situation correctly. We hold on to the offense to make sure that the offender gets his just punishment. But in the end, we do nothing but punish ourselves.

Are you holding any offenses against other people? For their sake and for yours, release those offenses to God. I know your mind thinks you are being a doormat if you do that, but you need to trust God to take care of the situation. Don't allow yourself to think, *If I trust God with these offenses, He will forgive those people and help them. But they need more than just forgiveness — they need to be punished!* Just forgive them, and let the matter drop. Let it go!

Peter asked Jesus how many times in a day we should forgive someone. Should it be seven? Jesus said, "No, it should be *seventy times seven*." That translates to 490 times a day! (Personally, I'd think that after about 180 times of forgiving someone in a single day, I might want to get away from that person!)

In Luke 17:1, Jesus said, *"...It is impossible that no offenses should come...."* That word "offenses" comes from the Greek word *scandalon*, which means *trap stick* or *bait stick*.[24]

Let me explain what that definition is talking about. In some countries, people eat monkeys. They have cages where

---

[24] Strong, "Greek Dictionary of the New Testament," #4625.

they leave the front door open. Inside the cage they put a bait stick or a trap stick — a *scandalon*. The monkey is too smart to go into the cage and get caught, so he goes around to the back of the cage and reaches through the bars to pick up the bait stick — which, of course, won't fit through the bars.

The monkey is smart enough not to go in through the front, but he is stubborn enough not to let the stick go. He holds on to the bait stick (offense) and keeps trying in vain to get it out. But the monkey will not let go of that stick, making it easy for the monkey hunter to come up and club the monkey and catch him.

Don't be like that monkey. You may think you'll never get caught in unforgiveness. You don't plan to get caught in that trap. After all, you love God and your fellow believers. But sometimes you still go in the back door of the trap. You grab hold of the offense (bait stick), and you have a hard time letting it go.

But is it worth going back into an old season of captivity just because you want to hold on to that offense? Jesus knows a lot more than you do, and He said to let it go.

So determine to keep short accounts in your life by getting rid of offense quickly. As soon as you realize you've taken offense, throw it down before you get clubbed by the enemy. Let it go! Freely give and freely receive forgiveness in this new season you've entered. There is no more effective way to sail on through unhindered to the next season of blessing that lies up ahead!

> ...Is it worth going back into an old season of captivity just because you want to hold on to that offense?

GET THE HELP YOU NEED

You need to always keep in mind that you didn't enter into this new season by yourself. You had help. Think about the times when you weren't serving God; yet still He saved you from your own foolishness. Where would you be without the Lord on your side? I'll tell you where — you'd have been swallowed up by the enemy!

Now that you're in a new season, there may still be times when you need to seek help — not only from God, but from other people. For instance, if you have deep-rooted issues or cycles of sin in your life, you may not have all the tools you need to rid yourself of these strongholds once and for all. If that is the case, realize that there is no shame at all in looking for help to get free. Yes, you're in a new season; yes, you're cleansed and happy. But those strongholds may come back to torment you when pressure comes your way.

So if there is an area of bondage that has corrupted every season of your life, go ahead and get help. Don't wait until a rough situation comes along before you decide to deal with the problem. You'll only make it harder on yourself.

Ecclesiastes 4:10 says, *"...woe to him who is alone when he falls, for he has no one to help him up."* There is nothing wrong with getting someone to help you. You may need counseling regarding your finances. You may need help from a doctor. You may need to go back to college and further your education. Or you may just need a good Christian friend who doesn't gossip!

A sweet, precious lady greeted me on the way out of the church after one Sunday morning service. When I told her to have a blessed day, she blurted out, "Pastor, I need help. I'm just back and forth, in and out, trying to stop smoking but with no real success." I told this woman the same thing I'm telling you: "There is no shame in looking for help to get free."

I remember another gentleman who came up to me at church and told me that he couldn't read and needed help. I could see that this man's inability to read was hindering his confidence in everyday life and limiting his job performance in the workplace. So I told him to call the church and we'd make sure he got in contact with someone who could help him. I gave him the same message: "There's no shame at all in getting help when you need it."

Christians may look cleaned up while they're at church, but many of them have deep-rooted issues, hurts, and dysfunctional ways to cope with the pressures of life. For instance, some people are as sweet as they can be, but inside they harbor volcanic anger that erupts when it's least expected. For other people, the deep-rooted issue lies in the area of finances. In every season of these people's lives, they have made some kind of financial mess. They almost succeed in getting out of debt — and then to celebrate, they go out and buy something big with their credit card, thus starting the process of building up debt all over again!

Sometimes the devil tries to heap such shame on people that they never seek help and they never get past their problems. They'd rather paint over their issues and let everyone think that everything is going great in their lives.

But it's time for us to get free from *all* forms of bondage. We need to realize that our flesh had its way for most of our lives and that our minds are not yet fully renewed as we continue to grow in the Lord. So there is absolutely nothing wrong with us getting the help we need so we don't find ourselves in the same sad situation we were trapped in before. We have to be willing to *get* free and to *stay* free in the new season we have entered by God's grace.

The nature of sin is this: It does *not* get better if you don't deal with it. It will just wait for an opportune time to grab you and gain an even greater hold on you than it had before. That's why you have to be set free completely from those sinful strongholds that have held you in bondage for so long.

> The nature of sin is this: It does *not* get better if you don't deal with it.

Allowing a stronghold to remain in your life is like never fixing a hole in the roof of your house. When it rains hard, your furniture and carpet will get ruined because of that hole. You can clean up the carpet and re-cover the furniture. You can invite everyone over to see how nice your "new season" looks. But what if you don't fix the hole in the roof because you don't have a tall enough ladder or the necessary tools and expertise? The next time it rains, your new season is going to end up looking a lot like the old season you just re-covered and cleaned up!

No, if you want your new season to keep looking new, you'll have to fix that hole in the roof — and to do that, you may need to reach out and ask for help.

That's what Naaman had to do in Second Kings 5. Naaman was a commander in the Syrian army, a mighty man of valor and a great warrior. However, Naaman was also a leper.

One day the Syrian army came back from a raid with some Israelite slaves they had captured. One of the slave girls was brought to Naaman's household to be a servant to his wife. This servant girl told Naaman's wife, "...*If only my master were with the prophet who is in Samaria! For he would heal him of his leprosy*" (v. 3).

What was the servant girl saying? She knew where Naaman could get some help. And because Naaman listened to this unlikely source of good counsel, he found the help he needed in the person of Elisha and was healed of his leprosy as he obeyed the prophet's instructions.

There are connections to be made to help you through your new season, friend. So if you need help, get it. You may be free right now, but you want to *stay* free. Therefore, you may need to uproot some harmful things from your life.

Never forget, however, that although God uses people, you must always look to God first. King Asa understood that. In Second Chronicles 14:11, Asa prayed, "...*Lord, it is nothing for You to help, whether with many or with those who have no power; help us, O Lord our God, for we rest on You, and in Your name we go against this multitude. O Lord, You are our God; do not let man prevail against You!*"

But two chapters later, Asa forgot his own prayer! When his feet became diseased, Asa didn't seek the Lord first. Instead, he sought his physician, and as a result, he died. Was there a problem with the physician? No, I believe all healing is from God. Asa just got the order of his priorities all wrong.

The principle is this: Ultimately, all your help comes from God, but sometimes God does use people. However, you are to seek God *first*. God will give you direction on how to get any other help that you need.

> **I lift up my eyes to the hills — where does my help come from?**
> **My help comes from the Lord, the Maker of heaven and earth.**
>
> **Psalm 121:1,2 NIV**

> **God is our refuge and strength, a very present help in trouble.**
>
> **Psalm 46:1**

> **Let us therefore come boldly to the throne of grace, that we may obtain mercy and find grace to help in time of need.**
>
> **Hebrews 4:16**

Regardless of any natural help you receive, God's grace is your ultimate source of help to draw on whenever you're facing a time of need.

My wife and I were riding together in the car recently, and she was driving. If Alicia gets cold from the car air conditioner, she turns the thermostat to 98 degrees Fahrenheit. If she gets hot, she turns it down to 34 degrees. On that particular day, she got cold, and turned the temperature to 104 degrees! I was reading when suddenly I could feel myself almost collapsing from the sudden blast of heat.

"Air!" I gasped. Why did I say that? Because air is what I needed!

Similarly, if our house was on fire, we'd shout, *"Water!"* So why do we shout "Grace, grace!" in the midst of our tests and trials? Because God's grace is what we need! God's grace will strengthen us on the inside and help us overcome in every situation of life.

Let me give you the bottom line: The same thing that got us out of the old season is what will *keep* us out of the old season. Therefore, our first line of action should be that same foundational principle: *We cried unto the Lord, and He heard our cry and delivered us.*

So call out to the Lord when you face problems and difficult situations. Don't immediately pick up the phone and call someone. The first thing you need to do is cry out to *God!*

Don't get in the mindset that you are in a new season and you can therefore just cruise along with no pressure or problems. Remember, the devil isn't celebrating your new season. He will constantly be looking for opportunities to lob obstacles onto your path, so you need to be ready for him.

Where does your help come from? Your help comes from the Lord. The same way you got out of the last season is the way you are going to get through this season. You *will* overcome, but you need to call upon God. As you do, He will hear, answer, and deliver you, leading you by His grace to the help you need so you can walk free and victorious into all the new seasons that are yet to come!

241

Living as an Overcomer In the New Seasons of Life

7

*I*t isn't enough to conduct yourself properly in a new season. God actually expects you to walk through life as more than a conqueror — a full-powered, faith-talking, devil-stomping overcomer in life!

Therefore, the final keys for conducting yourself properly in a new season are all wrapped up in the resurrection message. The same power that raised Jesus from the dead is the power God has provided for you so you can face every situation with confidence and overcome every challenge that comes your way.

YOU MUST HAVE POWER

You have to make a choice: Are you going to be a powerful Christian or a pitiful Christian? Anyone can be pitiful, but very few believers actually pay the price to tap into God's power in their daily walk with Him. You need to break out of the defeated mindset that is so common

> You have to make a choice: Are you going to be a powerful Christian or a pitiful Christian?

among Christians and determine that you're not only going to have power in your spiritual walk — you're going to be *full* of power!

I'm talking about the kind of power that comes from God, not a power that you muster up on your own. As you study the Scriptures, you'll find that this is the kind of divine power with which Jesus entered and left every season of His life on this earth.

For instance, when Jesus came out of the wilderness after spending forty days fasting and resisting the devil's temptations, He came out in the power of the Spirit (Luke 4:14). He didn't come out saying, "Wow, was it rough out there! Man, am I hungry! I'm telling you, the devil just would not leave Me alone!" Jesus didn't say any of that. He just returned in the power of the Spirit and began doing the works of the Father!

Everywhere Jesus went and all the good He did was according to the power and the anointing God had given Him. This is the message in Acts 10:38, which says, *"How God anointed Jesus of Nazareth with the Holy Spirit and with power, who went about doing good and healing all who were oppressed by the devil, for God was with Him."*

We, too, need God's power and life in order to live in this world victoriously. In Second Corinthians 12, the apostle Paul gives us the key to this power as he tells about a time he was buffeted by some difficult problems himself. Paul told the Lord in essence, "The devil won't let up on me, Lord. Can You help me with this?"

The Lord answered, "...*My grace is sufficient for you, for My strength is made perfect in weakness...*" (2 Cor. 12:9).

I'm so glad that when I am weak, Jesus is strong. It would be horrible if He was weak at the same time I was weak. Thank God, Jesus is *always* strong!

Paul "cuts to the chase" when he says in effect, "Our tendency as human beings is that when we are strong, we want to lean on our own strengths. We are so much better off when we say, 'God is my strength, my sole source of supply.'"

We need to lean on God and His grace, for His power manifests itself to its greatest capacity when we are weak. On the other hand, without the power of God, we are nothing more than pitiful mortal beings.

But I don't believe that we who are blood-bought children of the Most High God should be whimpering and limping through life in a pitiful fashion. We need to be full of power! Otherwise, we will violate the "truth-in-advertising" law, which is more true in God's Kingdom than it has ever been in our natural world!

GOD'S POWER MANIFESTED
AT THE CROSS AND THE TOMB

How great is God's power that is available to us as believers? We get a clue of its magnitude by looking at the many signs and supernatural manifestations of power surrounding Jesus' crucifixion and resurrection. Let's look at Matthew 27 in the *Message* translation to discover some of these demonstrations of divine power:

From noon to three, the whole earth was dark.

Around mid-afternoon Jesus groaned out of the depths, crying loudly, *"Eli, Eli, lama sabachthni?"* which means, "My God, my God, why have you abandoned me?"

Some bystanders who heard him said, "He's calling for Elijah."

One of them ran and got a sponge soaked in sour wine and lifted it on a stick so that he could drink.

The others joked, "Don't be in such a hurry. Let's see if Elijah comes and saves him."

But Jesus, again crying out loudly, breathed his last.

At that moment, the Temple curtain was ripped in two, top to bottom. There was an earthquake, and rocks were split in pieces.

What's more, tombs were opened up, and many bodies of believers asleep in their graves were raised.

(After Jesus' resurrection, they left the tombs, entered the holy city, and appeared to many.)

The captain of the guard and those with him, when they saw the earthquake and everything else that was happening, were scared to death. They said, "This has to be the Son of God!"

Matthew 27:45-54 *Message*

These were certainly supernatural manifestations of power! From noon to three, while Jesus hung on the Cross, it was dark — yet that is normally one of the hottest, brightest times of the day. And when Jesus gave up His spirit, the veil in the Temple — which was about *sixty feet* high and several inches thick — was torn from top to bottom. I guarantee you, *no one* could have gotten into the temple to fake *that* stunt!

This was the veil that separated the Presence of God from the holiest place that man was allowed to go in the temple. Until that moment, man was still separated from

God's Presence. But at the death of Jesus, that veil was torn in two from top to bottom, signaling loud and clear that not only could man enter the Presence of God, but now the Presence of God could come to man!

At that same moment in time, an earthquake erupted in the land, and great rocks were broken into pieces. Graves were opened up, and Old Testament believers came out of their tombs alive. In fact, after Jesus was raised from the dead, the Scriptures say these believers got up and went into town! Can you imagine being in the coffee shop reading the newspaper when that happened?

When the captain of the guard and those who were with him saw all these manifestations of God's power that were going on around them, they had one comment: "This *has* to be the Son of God!"

I can't prove what I'm about to say, but I think we'll find out it's true when we get to Heaven. I believe that on the Day of Pentecost, of the three thousand people who got saved, some of the first were those soldiers. They knew by what they witnessed on the day of Jesus' crucifixion that He had to be the Son of God.

There were also great demonstrations and manifestations of God's power surrounding Jesus' resurrection from the dead. We celebrate this event every year at Easter, but I don't think most of us comprehend the magnitude of what we're celebrating.

You see, Easter is about much more than just bunnies and baskets. For years as a little boy, I thought Easter was about hiding things. On Easter Sunday morning, we would get up and my mom would tell us to look for our baskets that she had hidden. Then after church, we would hunt for hidden Easter eggs. That's what Easter meant to me for the longest time. But the truth is this: Easter is not about hiding eggs; it's about *God's demonstrated power* — not just power that was available a long time ago, but power that is available *today*.

Ephesians 1 talks about this provision of divine power that is part of our spiritual inheritance:

> ...Therefore I also, after I heard of your faith in the Lord Jesus and your love for all the saints,
>
> do not cease to give thanks for you, making mention of you in my prayers:
>
> that the God of our Lord Jesus Christ, the Father of glory, may give to you the spirit of wisdom and revelation in the knowledge of Him,
>
> the eyes of your understanding being enlightened; that you may know what is the hope of His calling, what are the riches of the glory of His inheritance in the saints.

> **Ephesians 1:15-18**

Look at that phrase "the eyes of your understanding being enlightened" in verse 18. That's talking about *seeing with your heart*. Paul prayed this for the Ephesian believers because it is God's will that His people see and comprehend certain truths. One of the most important of these truths is found in verses 19-21:

> And what is the exceeding greatness of His power toward us who believe, according to the working of His mighty power
>
> which He worked in Christ when He raised Him from the dead and seated Him at His right hand in the heavenly places,
>
> far above all principality and power and might and dominion, and every name that is named, not only in this age but also in that which is to come.

Consider this: Psalm 19:1 says that creation and the universe were God's handiwork, or the works of His *hands*. The Bible goes on to say in about six different references that salvation and redemption was the work of His mighty *arm*. We can conclude, then, that it took more power for God to raise Jesus from the dead and accomplish our salvation and redemption than it did for Him to create the universe. That's pretty exciting!

Paul prayed that we'd be able to see with our hearts and come to know and understand the exceeding greatness of God's power toward us who believe. The *Amplified Bible* describes it as "...*the immeasurable and unlimited and surpassing greatness of His power...*" (Eph. 1:19).

This power is way beyond great — it is *exceeding* in its greatness! Nothing can stop this power! The Greek language words it this way: *to throw beyond the mark*.[25] In other words, compared to any mark ever made by a source of power, the power of God that is available to us goes *way* beyond that mark.

This kind of power never runs out but is always there when you need it. It isn't like a natural source of power that is eventually exhausted through use.

For instance, I have an armoire, which is a fancy word for a dresser with doors on it. In this armoire, I have a sock drawer. As a pastor, I often have to dress more formally, so I often wear one of my basic black, navy blue, or dark green suits. I like to match my socks to my suits; however, the socks are sometimes difficult to differentiate in color as they lie folded in my drawer. To make it even more difficult, it's usually dark when I'm getting ready for church on Sunday mornings.

---

[25] Ibid., #5235.

To solve this problem without waking my wife, I bought a small light that attaches to the drawer itself. The little light is supposed to illuminate my sock drawer; however, it doesn't work very well, so I usually use a flashlight. But sometimes the flashlight fades, and then I have two choices: turn on the bedroom light and wake up Alicia, or risk wearing one black sock and one dark green one!

I'm so glad that the kind of power God gives us isn't unreliable like the battery power I use to figure out what is in my armoire drawers! We never have to wonder if we'll have the power we need to overcome a situation we might face in the new season.

Most all of us know the frustration of getting into our car and turning the key, only to find out that the car won't start for some reason. But we never have to worry about that happening with the power that comes from God, for it's *always* there. Death and the devil couldn't stop that power when Jesus lay in that tomb. Doubt couldn't stop it. Armies and governments couldn't stop it. Centuries of sin and curse couldn't stop it. *Nothing* can stop the power of Almighty God when it is released to fulfill His purposes!

Not only can this power not be stopped, but it also never runs out. God's power was *not* all used up at the resurrection! He didn't have to save all winter to have enough power to raise Jesus from the dead. The resurrection was just the *release* of His mighty power flowing toward our lives. It was just the beginning!

> *Nothing* can stop the power of Almighty God when it is released to fulfill His purposes!

That divine power still flows just as abundantly today as it did on that first

Easter morning. And it is that power which will help you live victoriously through this new season and through every new season of life that awaits you on the road up ahead!

STAY PLUGGED IN
TO THE POWER SOURCE

God's power is waiting to help you do something. You have challenges coming up this week, and you'll need help overcoming them. There are situations coming you don't even know about yet, and you'll need help getting through them victoriously. You can't depend on your own strength and your own energy to get you through. You need help beyond yourself.

Fortunately, the same power God demonstrated when He raised Jesus from the dead is available to *you*! However, it's important to understand that this power is not automatic. You have to plug into it.

Have you ever put bread in your toaster and pushed down the button — but nothing happened? You get out the butter and the knife, and you wait. You pour your coffee and your juice, and you keep waiting. You get out your napkin and plate, and you wait some more. You're all ready for that toast, but nothing is happening. You look inside the toaster and realize that it isn't even hot. Then you look at the cord and figure out the problem — the toaster isn't even plugged in!

Is your problem a lack of electrical power? No, it's a lack of being plugged in. Forget trying to figure out who unplugged the toaster. You just need to plug the cord back in so you can enjoy the results of a renewed power flow!

In the same way, don't waste your time blaming the people who may have unplugged you over the course of your life. Just get plugged back in to God's power! What does it take to do that? For God's resurrection power to make any difference in your life, your circumstances, or your seasons, *you just need to believe.*

Believe that you've been plugged into that power all along. Believe that God's power is ready and waiting to change something in your life — to cause something to heat up, cool off, turn on, or go fast. That power is ready to help you do what you need to do in order to overcome in this new season you're in. It is always available to you, but it is not automatic.

Romans 10:9 holds the key to activating God's power for salvation: *"That if you confess with your mouth the Lord Jesus and believe in your heart that God has raised Him from the dead, you will be saved."* That same key holds true for every other area of life.

How did you get saved? By declaring with your mouth that Jesus is Lord, and by believing that God raised Him from the dead. That isn't difficult to do. Salvation doesn't require twelve weeks of Bible school or a week of perfect performance. It requires one simple thing — saying with your mouth what you believe in your heart: "I believe that God raised Jesus from the dead." As a result of that simple action of faith, you are saved.

It is also just that simple to activate God's power in the situations you face every day. Believe and you'll receive the power of God; doubt and you'll do without!

Look at what Paul said in Philippians 3:10 (*AMP*) about the resurrection power of God flowing into our lives:

> **[For my determined purpose is] that I may know Him [that I may progressively become more deeply and intimately acquainted with Him, perceiving and recognizing and understanding the wonders of His Person more strongly and more clearly], and that I may in that same way come to know the power outflowing from His resurrection [which it exerts over believers]....**

The power is still flowing from the resurrection, and it still exerts itself over the lives of believers. That power is available, but it is not automatic. Each believer has to make the deliberate choice to *believe*.

Sometimes our finite minds wonder what difference a little faith makes in causing God's power to come on the scene. We just can't fully figure it all out. But we don't have to figure it all out with our natural minds; we just have to believe. As we do, God's power will flow from the resurrection into our lives to help us walk through this new season as overcomers in every realm — spirit, soul, and body!

Romans 8:11 explains the effect God's power has on the physical realm:

> **But if the Spirit of Him who raised Jesus from the dead dwells in you, He who raised Christ from the dead will also give life to your mortal bodies through His Spirit who dwells in you.**

That phrase "give life to your mortal bodies" has to do with physical healing and energy. If God's power was sufficient to raise up Jesus' physical body when it had been tortured to death, it's certainly sufficient to give you the energy you need to overcome any challenge that might lie up ahead! You just need to keep believing that the power of God will keep you energetic, healthy, and whole as you seek to do His will in this season of your life.

You can't escape this fact: To operate in God's power in this life, you have to believe with your words, your heart, your thoughts, and your expectations. No matter how helpless you feel, you have to declare by faith, "I can do *all* things through Christ who strengthens me!" (Phil. 4:13).

Some people are waiting to see something before they believe. But that isn't how it works in God's Kingdom. You first believe in what God has promised, and then you see it manifested in your life. If you believe that God's power will help you, you'll see His power come on the scene. But if you're sitting around waiting for His power to manifest before you'll believe that it's available to you, you will fail to see it demonstrated in your life when you need it the most.

> To operate in God's power in this life, you have to believe with your words, your heart, your thoughts, and your expectations.

You have to get plugged in by believing, and you have to demonstrate your faith by your words. At some point you have to throw the lever on the inside of you and *speak what you believe*:

"I believe that God raised Jesus from the dead. I believe that power was released at the resurrection that is still flowing toward me today. God's power is available to me because I believe. His power will help me in my body. It will help me in my relationships. It will help me with my problems. It will help me let go of my past. It will help me overcome in my present. It will help me take hold of my future. I believe that God's power is exceeding in its greatness, and it is working now in me!"

As you speak forth words born of the faith in your heart, God's power will be released in your life to change what needs to be changed, strengthen what needs to be strengthened, and bring to pass that which He desires to bring to pass in your life!

So don't try to get through this season on your own — not even for a moment. You may feel strong right now, but you need to realize that the Source of your strength is *God*, not your own human ability. And I guarantee you this: A time *will* come when you feel helpless to deal with the situation that confronts you. At that moment, you will need a power beyond yourself in order to overcome.

That power was released at the resurrection of Jesus Christ, and it still exerts itself over believers today. That power is to be used for life on this turf, not for the life to come in Heaven. And that power is made available to *you* the moment you activate it by the faith-filled words of your mouth!

LOOK FOR THE NEW

New things grow in new seasons. So as you walk through this new season, keep expecting and looking for new things to grow.

God speaks of this principle in Isaiah 43:18,19:

"Do not remember the former things, nor consider the things of old.

Behold, I will do a new thing, now it shall spring forth; shall you not know it? I will even make a road in the wilderness and rivers in the desert."

The new crop of blessings won't come all at once, but it *will* come. So don't become "decrease-minded." If you are in a new season, give that new crop time to grow. According to Jesus' teaching in Mark 4:26-29, that's the way it works in the Kingdom of God.

> The new crop of blessings won't come all at once, but it *will* come.

And He said, "The kingdom of God is as if a man should scatter seed on the ground,
and should sleep by night and rise by day, and the seed should sprout and grow, he himself does not know how.
"For the earth yields crops by itself: first the blade, then the head, after that the full grain in the head.
"But when the grain ripens, immediately he puts in the sickle, because the harvest has come."

"...*First the blade, then the head, after that the full grain in the head*" (v. 28). In other words, the growth of the new — new blessings, new spiritual maturity, new levels of power — is a process. As Isaiah 28:13 says, it is a matter of "...*here a little, there a little....*" You just need to be patient, believing God for the new to spring forth in your life as you stay willing and obedient each step of the way.

The law of seedtime and harvest operates in every realm of life. We can see this in Isaiah 61:11:

For as the earth brings forth its bud, as the garden causes the things that are sown in it to spring forth, so the Lord God will cause righteousness and praise to spring forth before all the nations.

Every spring I plant my garden. In every row, I have different kinds of plants growing, such as green beans, pinto beans, Georgia collards, squash, two different kinds of cucumbers, pumpkins, tomatoes — and the list goes on. As soon as I plant those seeds in the soil, everything begins to grow.

Every morning, one of the first things I do is walk outside to my garden and look at it. What am I looking for in my garden? *I'm looking for the new.* After barely a week passes by, I can already see some sprouts peeking above the ground.

Can I eat out of the garden yet? No, but I'm thrilled with what I see. I praise God for that new growth, for it preaches to me every day. And as I keep looking for the new, I stay encouraged, blessed, and thankful as I look ahead to the harvest that I know is coming.

Of course, I can't get in pride about those little sprouts because the law of seedtime and harvest has been in place for a long, long time. Those seeds were already preprogrammed and prewired. The soil knows its part; the water knows its part; the sun knows its part; and the seed knows its part. God wired all these parts together within the law of seedtime and harvest long ago when He created the earth. All we do is cooperate with His system, knowing that over the course of time, our sowing by faith will produce the harvest we both desire and expect.

You have stepped into a new season. What's new in it? If your business wasn't doing well in the last season, start looking for new growth, new clients, new ideas. If you and your spouse have just been coexisting in your home, look for new sparks in your relationship. You can declare, "I think I just saw a sparkle in my mate's eye!"

We see this principle of looking for the new in First Kings 18:42-44, when Elijah began to pray for the end of a three-year drought in the land:

> ...And Elijah went up to the top of Carmel; then he bowed down on the ground, and put his face between his knees,
> and said to his servant, "Go up now, look toward the sea." So he went up and looked, and said, "There is nothing." And seven times he said, "Go again."
> Then it came to pass the seventh time, that he said, "There is a cloud, as small as a man's hand, rising out of the sea!" So he said, "Go up, say to Ahab, 'Prepare your chariot, and go down before the rain stops you.'"

Every time the servant came back and said there were no clouds, Elijah told him to go look again. Finally, the servant came back and said he had seen a tiny cloud the size of a man's hand. The prophet's response was one of faith: Elijah told his servant to go tell the king that it was about to flood! I like that attitude!

You are in a new season, and God plans on taking you from glory to glory. He's doing a new thing in your life. He's causing new blessings and new victory to come forth. You don't have to know how He's doing it. You just have to do your part by diligently looking for the new.

Jesus established a powerful principle when He said, "Seek and you will find" (Luke 11:9). What you are looking for, you will find. But it's up to you to apply that principle to your life in the right way. Don't look for things to go bad or to slide backwards in reverse. Look for blessing, increase, wholeness, strength, happiness, and breakthrough. When you do that, you'll begin to see the new that you've been looking for. Your expectation will act like a magnet to bring it into your life by the power of God.

Here is something else you need to understand about this particular key to proper conduct in a new season: *There is no age limit on looking for the new.* Psalm 92:12-14 confirms this:

> The righteous shall flourish like a palm tree, he shall grow like a cedar in Lebanon.
> Those who are planted in the house of the Lord shall flourish in the courts of our God.
> They shall still bear fruit in old age; they shall be fresh and flourishing.

There is also no past hardship or calamity that can prevent you from looking for the new in this season of your life. According to Isaiah 61:1-7 (*NIV*), Jesus came to comfort those who mourn and give them "beauty for ashes" — and that includes anything that has happened in your past.

> The Spirit of the Sovereign Lord is on me, because the Lord has anointed me to preach good news to the poor. He has sent me to bind up the brokenhearted, to proclaim freedom for the captives and release from darkness for the prisoners,
> to proclaim the year of the Lord's favor and the day of vengeance of our God, to comfort all who mourn,
> and provide for those who grieve in Zion — to bestow on them a crown of beauty instead of ashes, the oil of gladness instead of mourning, and a garment of praise instead of a spirit of despair. They will be called oaks of righteousness, a planting of the Lord for the display of his splendor.
> They will rebuild the ancient ruins and restore the places long devastated; they will renew the ruined cities that have been devastated for generations.

Aliens will shepherd your flocks; foreigners will work your fields and vineyards.

And you will be called priests of the Lord, you will be named ministers of our God. You will feed on the wealth of nations, and in their riches you will boast.

Instead of their shame my people will receive a double portion, and instead of disgrace they will rejoice in their inheritance; and so they will inherit a double portion in their land, and everlasting joy will be theirs.

In Zion, which is the Church, there are people who are mourning. Proverbs 5:14 says that there are people on the verge of total ruin in the midst of the congregation, even though they may look all shined up as they make their way to church. God is aware of this, and He has promised that He would console those who mourn in Zion.

If you are going through something today, there is a next step that God wants to show you. He also wants to comfort and console you. He knows what you're going through. He doesn't expect you to "get it all together" by tomorrow at noon. He just wants you to let Him help you begin the process of getting it all together!

So begin looking for the new. Look for it in your marriage, your family, your health, your finances, your church, and your life. As you do, you'll begin to see what you've been looking for. God said, "I will do a new thing." He brought you *out* so He could bring you *into* a new season where you could learn to live in the fullness of His promises to you.

You can look at whatever you want to look at. You can look for whatever you want to look for. But if you start looking for the new, it will start showing up. It's your choice. You can make this principle work for your benefit.

Do what God tells you to do. Honor His principles, and then watch what happens!

> ...If you start looking for the new, it will start showing up. It's your choice.

You won't understand *how* those new little plantings of faith start growing toward a future harvest, but you don't have to. You can just be happy that new little sprouts of victory are showing up all around you as you look forward to eating the fruit of your obedience!

POWER TO WALK
IN THE NEWNESS OF LIFE

The power of God will even help you behave wisely in this new season. You see, God doesn't control you, but He does give you the power to control yourself. His power will help you walk in the newness of life as He has called you to do. If you say you can't do that on your own, you're absolutely right. But if you will believe that God's power will help you, it most certainly will.

This is the wonderful message of hope proclaimed in these two New Testament scriptures:

> **We were buried therefore with Him by the baptism into death, so that just as Christ was raised from the dead by the glorious [power] of the Father, so we too might [habitually] live and behave in newness of life.**
>
> **Romans 6:4 *AMP***

> **I have been crucified with Christ; it is no longer I who live, but Christ lives in me; and the life which I**

now live in the flesh I live by faith in the Son of God, who loved me and gave Himself for me.

Galatians 2:20

There was a power released at the Resurrection that will help you overcome your yesterdays — *if* you will believe. That same power will also help you live as an overcomer today and tomorrow — *if* you will believe.

This is what it all comes down to: By believing, you allow the Holy Spirit to live big *in* you and to deal with your challenges *through* you. It will still be you talking, acting, moving, and deciding, but the Holy Spirit will show you what to do, when to do it, where to go, how fast to go, when to take a sharp left turn, and when to stop. He'll teach you and help you through every season of life, giving you the grace to get through the most difficult challenges victoriously.

I'd like to be able to say that you won't have to face difficult situations in your new season or in the seasons to come. Certainly none of us desire difficulties and problems in life. Nevertheless, the fact remains that we all face tests and trials at one time or another.

> By believing, you allow the Holy Spirit to live big *in* you and to deal with your challenges *through* you.

These are the times you need to tap into the divine power that continually flows toward you, just waiting to be released through the faith-filled words of your mouth.

How do you conduct yourself in a new season? By now you should have a clear idea, for you hold in your hand a good number of the most important keys found in the Scriptures.

Don't ever let go of these scriptural truths. They will not only take you through this present season in victory, but they will also unlock future seasons of blessing still hidden in the mind of God. Remember — there is a future and a hope to lay hold of, more doorways of opportunity to go through, and a broad, open land of promise that you have yet to explore!

PRAYER OF SALVATION

*H*ave you opened up the door of your heart to Jesus? Is He the Savior and Lord of your life?

Perhaps you have never invited Jesus to be your personal Savior, but you want to do that right now. If so, I encourage you to pray this prayer from your heart and speak it out of your mouth. As you do, God will hear you and answer your prayer.

> Father God, I come to You now in the Name of Jesus. Jesus, You loved me enough to give Yourself for me, so right now I give myself to You. I ask You to come into my heart and my life and be my Savior and Lord.

> Forgive me right now of every sin. Cleanse me from all unrighteousness by Your blood that was shed for me. Make me brand new and fill me with Your peace, with Your joy, with Your Holy Spirit, and with the assurance that You'll never leave me nor forsake me. I thank You now for answering my prayer. In Jesus' Name, amen.

PRAYER OF CONSECRATION

I encourage you to take a little time to check on the inside and see how you're doing with God. Are there any areas of your life in which you need to get right with the Lord? Are you sure Jesus is on the throne of your heart?

God knows where you are at; He knows what's going on in your life. He loves you and wants to help you. With this in mind, I urge you to pray this prayer of consecration. Then just believe God to go to work on your behalf as you take your hands off your circumstances and determine to trust in Him.

> Father God, I declare that You are the Most High God, my Creator, my Redeemer, and my Deliverer. Your thoughts and ways are higher than my thoughts and ways; therefore, I trust Your plans for my life. I thank You that You bring me *out* so You might bring me *into* all that You have purposed for my life.

Right now I acknowledge and repent of anything in my life that is not pleasing in Your sight. I renounce these sinful things, and I ask You now by the blood of Jesus to thoroughly cleanse me, forgive me, and make me brand new.

I thank You, Father, for doing that. I also thank You for helping me in the days ahead should any of these strongholds try to resurface in my life. If that happens, I determine right now to knock every one of them back down by Your power so that I am not hindered from entering into all that You have for me. In Jesus' Name, amen.

ABOUT THE AUTHOR

*I*n August 1989, Tim Gilligan and his wife Alicia came to Ocala, Florida, to establish Ocala Word of Faith Church. The first service was held at the Ocala Hilton Conference Center with approximately fourteen people in attendance. Since then, Ocala Word of Faith Church continues to grow with a current weekly attendance of nearly 4,000.

This growth can be attributed to the sound biblical teaching that Pastor Tim gives with great clarity and conciseness. As a teacher of God's Word, he emphasizes and illustrates the simple truths of God's promises, which are the keys to victory in every area of life.

Pastor Tim is ordained with the Association of Faith Churches and Ministers (AFCM) and is the Regional Director for Florida and the Caribbean. With the wisdom of God, Tim is used mightily in assisting other pastors in church administration and in giving spiritual guidance to ministers.

Other Books and Tapes By Tim Gilligan

Books:

Playing for Keeps — $10.00
Your Word and Your Work — $4.00

Audio Tapes:

Angers Away (4 tapes) $16.00
Communication That Counts (7 tapes) $28.00
Marriage Matters (7 parts) — on CD: $35:00; 7 tapes: $28.00
Seasons (17 parts) — on CD: $85.00; 17 tapes: $68.00
Recovering All (6 tapes) $24.00
Faith That Works (3 tapes) $12.00
Supply of the Spirit (13 tapes) $52.00
Finished With Fear (7 tapes) $28.00
A Question of Identity (8 tapes) $32.00
The Force of Endurance (6 tapes) $24.00
Reasons for Rest (7 parts) — on CD: $35.00; 7 tapes: $28.00
The Ocean of Emotion (14 parts) — on CD: $70.00;
   14 tapes: $56.00

FOR FURTHER INFORMATION

For additional copies of this book
or for further information
regarding Tim Gilligan's ministry schedule,
please write:

Pastor Tim Gilligan
Ocala Word of Faith Church
4741 SW 20th Street
Ocala, FL 34474
(352) 873-3767

*Please include your prayer requests
and comments when you write.*